Short-Sale Pre-Foreclosure Investing

Short-Sale Pre-Foreclosure Investing

How to Buy "No-Equity" Properties
Directly from the Bank—
at Huge Discounts

Dwan Bent-Twyford
Sharon Restrepo

WILEY
John Wiley & Sons, Inc.

Published by John Wiley & Sons, Inc., Hoboken, New Jersey.
Published simultaneously in Canada.

For general information on our other products and services or for technical support, please contact our Customer Care Department within the United States at (800) 762-2974, outside the United States at (317) 572-3993 or fax (317) 572-4002.

Wiley also publishes its books in a variety of electronic formats. Some content that appears in print may not be available in electronic books. For more information about Wiley products, visit our web site at www.wiley.com.

Library of Congress Cataloging-in-Publication Data:

Bent-Twyford, Dwan, 1959–
    Short-sale pre-foreclosure investing : how to buy "no-equity" properties directly from the bank—at huge discounts / Dwan Bent-Twyford, Sharon Restrepo.
        p.   cm.
    Includes index.
    ISBN 978-0-470-29030-9 (pbk.)
    1. Real estate investment—United States.   2. Foreclosure—United States.   3. Real property—Purchasing—United States.   I. Restrepo, Sharon.   II. Title.
HD255.B46   2008
332.63'24—dc22

                                                                                    2008009615

Printed in the United States of America.

10   9   8   7   6   5   4   3   2

CONTENTS

DOWNLOADABLE FORMS   ix

ACKNOWLEDGMENTS   xi

INTRODUCTION   xiii

CHAPTER 1   **Get Motivated, Set Goals, Get Started**   1

A Short-Sale Case Study—with a $200,000 Profit   2
Getting Motivated   6
Setting Goals   7
Accomplishing Your Goals   9
This Is a Business, Not a Hobby   10
Dealing with Naysayers   10
Personal Appearance   12
Setting Up Your Office   13
Structuring Your Business   14
Ready to Do Business   16

CHAPTER 2   **What Is a Short-Sale? An Executive
Summary of How to Negotiate with the
Bank and the Homeowner**   19

Why Do I Need to Do a Short-Sale?   20
Why Do Banks Accept Short-Sales?   21
How Much Do You Offer the Bank?   23
Successful Short-Sales Start with the Homeowner   33
Financial Agreement with the Homeowners   33
How Much Should You Pay the Homeowner to Move?   35
Setting the Move-Out Date   36

CHAPTER 3   **Expert Strategies for Finding
Distressed Properties and Foreclosures**   39

Buying Bank-Owned Properties for Pennies on the Dollar   39
Newspaper Ads   43
"I Buy Houses for Cash" Street Signs   44
Networking   44
Postcards   45
Magnetic Vehicle Signs   45

	Bail Bondsmen	46
	Pawnshops	46
	More Deal-Finding Favorites	49

CHAPTER 4   **How to Approach the Homeowners and Create a Win-Win Solution**   51

Understanding Why Homeowners Want to Work with You	52
Building Courage to Knock on Doors	53
Friendly Negotiations with the Homeowners—What to Say and What You Need from Them	54
Establishing Rapport over the Phone	57
Knock on Doors Like a Pro	57
Helping Homeowners Understand Their Options	59
Deed in Lieu of Foreclosure	64
Chapter 13 Bankruptcy	65
Final Thoughts	65

CHAPTER 5   **Preparing Your First Offer**   69

Authorization to Release Information	75
Going to Contract	79
Hardship Letter	88
Pictures	98
Investor Cover Letter	99
Comps That Justify Your Offer	101
Net Sheet	105
Estimated List and Cost of Repairs	107

CHAPTER 6   **How to Approach the Bank**   113

How to Get the Bank Interested in Talking to You	114
What the Bank Wants from an Investor	114
How to Get Through to a Stonewalling Lender	115
Presenting Your Short-Sale Offer to the Bank	115
The Asset Manager's Role	119
Working with the Portfolio Representative Directly	121
Getting Your Short-Sale Assigned to a Loss Mitigation Rep	121
Additional Information the Bank May Require	122
My Offer Is Submitted—Now What?	127

CHAPTER 7   **Negotiating with a Second or Third Mortgage Holder**   131

Your Conversation with the Second Lender	136
Variations on a Theme	139

CHAPTER 8   **Key Elements of the Legal Process You Must Understand**   145

Understanding Ownership versus Debt   146
Foreclosure Process   149
Types of Liens   152
Types of Mortgages and Loans   155

CHAPTER 9   **When the Bank Says Yes**   159

How Do I Buy More Time?   162
How Does the Homeowner Buy More Time?   163

CHAPTER 10   **Three Profit-Making Exit Strategies: Wholesaling, Rehabbing, and Renting**   169

The Wholesale Path   170
The Rehab Path   173
Selling the Home   180
The Rental Path   180

CHAPTER 11   **Setting the Closing Date and Making Sure the Closing Goes Smoothly**   183

A Successful Closing   185
What If My Homeowners Change Their Minds?   186
What If My Buyers Change Their Minds?   189
Closing with the Assignment of Contract   191
Double or Simultaneous Closings   196
Are Double Closings Illegal?   198

CHAPTER 12   **First-Year Expectations**   201

How You Can Become Rich without Going to College   204
What We Did to Get Here   205
What You Can Expect in Your First Year   207
Thinking Like a Millionaire   208

INDEX   209

Figure 2.7	Sample Bill of Sale	35
Figure 3.1	Sample Letter of Intent	42
Figure 5.18	Sample Acquisition Phone Log	89
Figure 5.19	Sample Release Authorization Form	90
Figure 5.20	Sample Contract Information	91
Figure 5.21	Sample Contract for Sale and Purchase	92
Figure 5.22	Sample Homeowner Hardship Letter	98
Figure 5.25	Sample Cover Letter	102
Figure 5.26	Sample Net Sheet	106
Figure 5.27	Sample Repairs List	108
Figure 5.28	Sample Property Information Sheet	109
Figure 7.1	Sample Letter to Junior Lien Holder #1	140
Figure 7.2	Sample Letter to Junior Lien Holder #2	141
Figure 7.3	Sample Letter to Junior Lien Holder #3	142
Figure 7.4	Sample Hardship Letter from Distressed Homeowner	143
Figure 11.1	Sample Agreement for Assignment of Contract	192

Dwan's Acknowledgments

First, I want to thank Jesus for all His blessings. Next, my wonderful daughter, Ayla, who was my original inspiration and motivation to become a successful real estate investor. My desire to give her a good life led to my unstoppable attitude. I can proudly say that she has never spent one day in day care, and has traveled more than any teenager I know. We have a special bond, second to none. I also want to thank my fantastic husband, Bill. Along with Bill came two bonus kids, Kris and Billy, whom I love very much. We are a wonderfully blended family of five. God has truly blessed us by bringing us all together.

I also want to thank my fantastic business partner, Sharon Restrepo, for her insights, stories, and support through the years. We have achieved a high level of success by working with each other!

In addition, I want to thank my Mom, Dad & Lois, along with Cindy, Tom, Sarah, and Paul, for all their support. They always encourage me, no matter what I choose to do or how crazy my ideas may seem.

Thank you to the rest of my wonderful family, friends, and employees who helped me accomplish this goal in my life of writing a book. I could not do all the things I do without each and every one of you. I thank my students as well, as without you I'd have nothing to write about! I thank each one of you for your public display of support. I sincerely hope you make a million bucks this year!

Sharon's Acknowledgments

Where do I begin? First and foremost, I must say thank you to God! I thank my awesome family for all of their support in every one of my questionable endeavors. Thank you, Mom, Beverly, Fred, Jordan, Kirsten, and Sydney.

Second, I must thank Dwan and Juan (talk about a tongue twister!). Dwan, you have done so many crazy deals with me. I remember when we practiced teaching to an empty room just to get prepared for our dreams to come true. Our teaching ultimately led to the introduction into my life of my husband, Juan. Juan, you are an absolute dream come true, and I am extremely blessed to share my life and dreams with you, and most recently our new son, Joshua.

Last, I want to thank all of the Florida Real Estate Investors Association (FLREIA) members, as well as our students across the country, for allowing us to be part of your dreams' pursuit. And if you're reading this book, I thank you and look forward to finding out how it changes your life.

May God bless each and every one of you.

"It sounds like you are taking advantage of people in distress—are you?"

This is the first question many people ask when they find out what business we're in. Investors, we're here to tell you that you are *not* taking advantage of the homeowners. The homeowners find themselves in a desperate situation and see no way out. Something in their lives has changed—loss of a job, illness, death in the family, a job transfer, or something else along those lines. If someone does not step up to the plate and do something, the homeowners will lose their home, have a foreclosure on their credit report, and need at least seven years to get back on track. We are offering a solution, right now, that will allow the distressed sellers a fresh start. By letting us handle a short-sale of their property, they will have money to move, no foreclosure on their credit report, and a chance to buy a new home again.

Most homeowners tell us that we are "angels sent straight from God." We offer a solution to a problem that most folks never imagined they would encounter. No one grows up intending to be in financial distress someday. We want to be doctors, firefighters, and police officers when we are kids. Then something happens—we grow up and life takes over! We graduate from high school or college, take a job, and assume everything will work out. Unfortunately, it doesn't always work out for everyone.

We use this business as a ministry. We talk to homeowners about a fresh start and offer sincere encouragement. This business has been a blessing for both of us, and we know it will be for you, too.

This is such an amazing way to earn a terrific living!

We love it for two reasons:

1. We get to help homeowners get a fresh start.
2. We get to help *you* get a fresh start.

We don't know which we like better—getting a testimonial letter from a student with a copy of a $100,000 check attached or watching the look of joy on a homeowner's face when he or she realizes the nightmare is over. We feel so truly blessed to be in the position to do both. Investors, we know you will love this business as much as we do.

Get started now . . . and start living your dreams!

Why Is America in Foreclosure?

Why did the real estate market change so dramatically in 2007? Is it still a good idea to invest in real estate? When is the market going to turn around? Should I sell the properties I own before the prices drop again? Questions like these may have been on your mind recently. It's important to understand why the real estate market crashed in 2007, so you can ride the wave of opportunity it created. Let us clarify that this is a chance to take advantage of opportunity, *not* people. This business needs more investors with heart, who are trustworthy and desire to earn a great living creating winning situations for all parties.

The biggest reason for so many foreclosures and bankruptcies has been subprime, interest-only, or exotic loans. These loans are very appealing. Many of them are adjustable-rate mortgages (ARMs) that allow homeowners to purchase a larger house with a smaller initial payment rate. The problem is that when the payment rate changes, many folks cannot afford the larger payment and end up in foreclosure. Also, many people were allowed to take on greater monthly payments than they could handle, especially if they later on ran into financial trouble.

Let's take a look at several of these loans:

➤ *Teaser adjustable-rate mortgages.* These loans entice borrowers by promising an initial period of very low interest (typically around 1 percent to 2 percent), which later resets to market rates. Over two million borrowers will be jolted back to reality this year when their introductory periods begin to expire. Payments on a typical $200,000 loan at 2 percent are approximately $725 a month; at 7 percent, the payment is $1,340. If the property was purchased based on the affordability of a $725 monthly mortgage payment, what happens when the payment climbs to $1,340?

➤ *Subprime adjustable-rate mortgages.* Because many of these subprime or nonprime loans require no income verification, they attract low-income people or those with bad or marginal credit. These folks assume that they can't qualify for a more reasonable rate, so they take what they can get. Many are in questionable financial positions to begin with and are therefore in greater danger of defaulting. Subprime ARMs start with a lower interest rate that continues to climb each year. Homeowners can find themselves paying 13 percent interest in just a few short years. If the initial interest rate of 7 percent was the maximum payment they could afford, what do they do now?

➤ *Option adjustable-rate mortgages.* This type is initially the most appealing loan. It gives homeowners the choice each month of paying the principal and interest, just the interest, or an even smaller minimum amount. If the mortgage payment is $1,000 a month and the homeowners decide to pay $450, the balance of the payment goes on the back of the loan, causing negative amortization. Eighty percent of homeowners with these loans pay the bare minimum. Because the amount paid does not cover the amount due, the balance added to the back of the loan increases the total amount owed. Once the loan balance has increased to a certain point, the bank demands that the homeowners begin to make full payments on the now larger amount.

In the year 2000, only 19 percent of all new loans were exotic; in 2006 over 81 percent were. This tells us that most Americans own a property they can't afford. In addition, the income versus debt ratio has taken a dramatic swing.

In 2000:

➤ Fully 93 percent of mortgage payments consumed less than 36 percent of a homeowner's paycheck.

➤ Seven percent of mortgage payments consumed 36 percent or more of the homeowner's paycheck.

Let's take a look at what's been happening. We think you'll agree with us that these numbers are scary. In 2006:

➤ Only 33 percent of mortgage payments consumed less than 36 percent of a homeowner's paycheck.

➤ About 20 percent of mortgage payments consumed 36 percent to 58 percent of the paycheck.

➤ Fully 47 percent of mortgage payments consumed more than 58 percent of the homeowner's paycheck!

Almost half of all homeowners use more than half of their paychecks just to make their mortgage payments. This leaves very little left over for emergencies. In addition, when that payment increases due to an ARM rate hike, they can't afford it, resulting in a foreclosure. Finally, in some areas of the country, homeowners have incurred a hike in property taxes, insurance rates, and association fees, making it even harder for them to afford the monthly payment.

What does this mean to investors? It means there are unlimited properties available right now if you know what to do with them. If you can be a landlord, buy as many properties as you can afford that will give you positive cash flow. With the changing market, buy low and plan to hold for the long haul.

If you don't want to be a landlord, and if your local market is a buyer's market (meaning there is more than six months' worth of inventory available), offer incentives to get properties sold quickly: sell below market, offer no payments for 12 months, offer to pay all closing costs, offer new appliances, offer cash back at closing, and so on. Any property will sell if it is priced right, even in a buyer's market. Remember, 90 percent of the marketing is done when you set the price on the home.

The bottom line is that there has never been a better time to be a real estate investor. Foreclosures have skyrocketed because of exotic loans, and banks are being forced to accept short-sales in order to get rid of properties. With 50 percent of loans maxed out, banks no longer have a choice. Investors who know how to make money with short-sales will do extremely well.

What Is a Short-Sale?

Everywhere you turn, there is another seminar, another guru, or another boot camp, all teaching different ways to do short-sales. Can so many people be right? How many different ways can there be to do the same thing? Folks, there are not 100 different ways to do short-sales; there is one way, and everyone is trying to put a spin on it to seem original.

Since we were the first to introduce the short-sale strategy to the U.S. investing community, it's exciting to see how this strategy has exploded. We're going to review the short-sale concept and show you just how easy it actually is.

Completing a short-sale is not difficult: Through simple negotiations you get the bank to accept less than what is owed on a property. For example, you find a homeowner with a property worth $100,000 that has a $100,000 mortgage balance. You work with the bank to negotiate a discount on the payoff. The bank agrees to accept $50,000 as payment in full. You have just completed your first short-sale.

The Four Parties Involved in a Short-Sale

Is it really that simple? You bet! The key to successful short-sales is to understand the mind-sets of the people involved and make the deal appealing to each of them. There are basically four parties involved in a successful short-sale: you the investor, the homeowner who is interested in getting out of foreclosure, the bank that wants to get a bad debt off its books, and the rehabber or landlord who buys the property from you at a discount. Of course, you can choose to hang on to the property and do the rehab yourself, and then rent it out or sell it for retail. In each situation, there is a win-win outcome.

Let's start with the homeowners. Their motivation is obvious. They are behind in payments or already in foreclosure. They are getting called by creditors, banks, attorneys, mortgage brokers, and more every day. They just want to be able to sleep at night and get out from under the stress this situation has placed on their lives. Their downfall is that they have no equity. They have called every investor in town to try to sell their house and have been turned down by everyone because they have no equity. They call you and you say, "No equity? No problem!" You explain the short-sale concept, get the property under contract, and get busy.

Why would the bank accept less than it is owed on a property? After all, the bank could take the property back at the sheriff's sale and then sell it for a retail price. Well, let us ask you this: Are banks in the business of lending money or owning homes? Correct, lending money. Is a foreclosure an asset or a liability? Right again, a liability.

Banks are in the business of wholesaling money. They borrow money from bigger banks and then lend it to you. They have to show their credit report, just like you do, to get a low interest rate on the money they are trying to borrow. If you were going to lend millions of dollars to a bank, would you lend your money to the banks with the low default rates or the banks with the high default rates? Of course, you would lend to the banks with the smallest number of defaulted or foreclosable loans. The bank's motivation to accept a short-sale is to clean up its books so that it can borrow more money, at a cheaper rate, and then lend it to you.

Where do rehabbers and landlords come into play? If you don't want to fix up a property yourself or keep it, you need someone to flip the property to once you negotiate a successful short-sale. Rehabbers and landlords are the perfect outlet. Rehabbers like to purchase fixer-uppers at no more than 65 percent of the retail value. Landlords like to buy at no more than 80 percent of the retail value. In the case of the $100,000 property, a rehabber wants to buy it for no more than $65,000 while a landlord might pay as much as $80,000.

So, how do you get the bank to say yes? You build a great case. Think of it like an attorney defending a case. The better case you build, the better your chances are to win. We send as much information as we possibly can to the bank to show the bank why it should accept our low offer now instead of waiting months to creep through the foreclosure and bankruptcy process and get the house later.

How do you build a good case? Send the following:

➤ A sales contract, signed by the homeowners, for the amount you want to offer the bank.
➤ An "Authorization to Release Information" form.
➤ Comparable sales (comps) that justify your offer.
➤ Pictures of all the disrepair.
➤ A detailed list of repairs needed.
➤ A hardship letter written by the homeowners, backed up with proof such as late notices, shutoff notices, bank statements, job layoff papers, medical bills, tax returns, or whatever you can find.
➤ Reports of crime in the neighborhood.

➤ A list of sex offenders in the area.

➤ Newspaper articles showing negative trends that could hurt real estate prices: job layoffs, crime, natural disasters, foreclosures up, bankruptcies up, and whatever you can find that is detrimental to the neighborhood.

➤ Net sheet showing what the bank would receive after closing costs.

➤ A cover letter from you stating why you couldn't possibly pay full price for the property.

Submit that information to the loss mitigation department of the bank, and you are in business. The rep will negotiate with you, and once you settle on a price, you can wholesale the property to the rehabber. You become the intermediary and keep the difference between what you negotiated with the bank and the rehabber.

Folks, short-sales are that easy. There are millions of dollars being left on the table. Get busy and put some of that money in your pocket. We are going to show you how.

The Authors' Stories: How We Got Started

Dwan's Story

Throughout my adult life I worked an endless string of dead-end jobs ranging anywhere from waiting tables at Denny's, to selling vitamins on the phone, to owning a tanning salon. Most of the jobs paid okay, but were unrewarding and required me to work many hours. I went from job to job, looking for something that I could really sink my teeth into, without much success. I thought I had found it with the tanning salon. As it turned out, I was tied to the salon seven days a week. Every weekend, when one of my girls called in sick, guess who had the privilege of working? Right . . . me. I got to the point where I hated the business because of the insane hours. I went for two years with hardly a day off. I decided to sell the business and get my life back.

Around this time I met a man and decided to get married, have babies, and be a stay-at-home mom. At 29, I had a baby on the way and life was looking pretty good. But things happen, and a year later I found myself going through a divorce with an eight-month-old daughter to care for. Life as a single mom had definitely not been in my game plan.

As a result of this very messy situation, I had no money, no car, no job, and $75 in the bank. It was a bleak state of affairs. I had to borrow money from an aunt to buy a car so I could job hunt. I desperately needed to go back to work, but the idea of leaving my daughter in day care, working for someone else all week, and then paying my hard-earned money to the day-care center was unacceptable. This just was not a sacrifice I was willing to make! I needed a new game plan, and I needed it fast.

As fate would have it, around this time I met a group of guys who seemed to be leading a pretty leisurely life—golf every day, always traveling, constantly going out and spending money. You name it, they were doing it. It turned out that they were real estate investors. I had found what I was looking for. Being a real estate investor would allow me the freedom to work from home and raise my daughter myself. I learned as much as I could and went for it.

I bought my first dumpy fixer-upper and went to town on it. I became such a regular at Home Depot and asked so many questions that when the guys saw me coming, they would run the other way. They knew if they stopped to answer "just one quick question," I would keep them for an hour asking detailed questions about my next step of rehab. I took all of the weekend classes they offered, learned what I could, and got my rehab under way. I did all the rehab on the property myself: paint, tile, plumbing, you name it. I started to see a light at the end of the tunnel. The more I worked, the better my property looked.

After the repairs were completed, I put the house on the market, sold it *four* days later, made over $20,000 on my first deal, and never looked back!

When I worked my dead-end jobs, I would work all year long to make $20,000. To make that in one deal, working from home and having my daughter by my side, was a dream come true. I decided at that moment that real estate investing was for me. But I never dreamed it would turn into such an amazing career!

After three years as a rehabber, I began to get burned out on all the physical work it required from me. I was tired of being dirty all the time and breaking my back every day. At this point in my career, I had several handymen who helped me, but I wasn't able to do as many deals as I really wanted to. I knew there had to be a better way to make money in real estate.

I soon discovered wholesaling. I still helped homeowners in distress, but instead of rehabbing the properties myself, I flipped them to other rehabbers. Although I made a smaller fee on each deal, I was selling many more houses. I was thrilled! I wholesaled 75 properties my first year and knew I had found the answer to my problem.

In order to be a successful wholesaler, you must have properties with **equity**.

Equity The difference between what a homeowner owes and the value of the property. For example, a homeowner with a $100,000 property who owes $60,000 has $40,000 in equity.

Over the years, we noticed that fewer and fewer people had sufficient equity for us to wholesale as many properties as we wanted to. Our deals were getting tighter and tighter. One day we were at a closing and the bank sent over the payoff for more than expected with the final figures. Needless to say, we were very upset. Not sure what to do, we called the bank and stated that if they didn't remove the unexpected fees, the deal was off. Within a few minutes, the bank called back and agreed to a discount. We were stunned and the deal closed as scheduled.

We thought about what had happened for a few days and decided that if it worked once, it might work again. We set a plan in motion and at our next closing we called the bank and asked to have several thousand dollars' worth of fees waived. The bank agreed! We knew we were onto something. From that closing on, we called the bank every time to ask for a waiver of fees.

As we began seeing thousands of dollars waived at our closings, we wondered what would happen if we called the bank a few days before the closing and asked for a larger discount, and hence short-sales began. Over the years, we got braver and braver and asked for larger and larger discounts until we were buying properties at 50 percent of their value. At the time, we were the only investor we knew of who was doing short-sales.

FIGURE I.1   Dwan and Hubby

As we began making a dent in the real estate market in South Florida, other investors started asking us to teach them the secrets of our success. One thing led to another, and soon we were teaching nationwide.

Several years ago, I was teaching at a three-day convention in Colorado when I met a great guy. We struck up a conversation, went on a date a few weeks later, and got married! (See Figure I.1.) The funny thing is I had sworn I would never date an investor. I figured that I already ate, slept, and drank real estate and didn't want to spend all my free time talking about it as well. Life has a funny way of bringing you exactly what you need even if it's not what you think you want.

Along with Bill came two bonus kids, so now we are a family of five. We spend our time teaching, doing deals, and spoiling the kids. You never know what can happen by getting involved in real estate. I now have money and a man. I can't help you with men, but I can certainly help you make money!

After all these years in the business, I still love it. I love to do deals, and I love to teach new investors how to become successful. Honestly, nothing gives me greater joy than to receive letters from students who have just closed their first deal and earned a huge check. I get tears reading the letters I receive. I am humbled that this book may be the tool you use to change your financial future.

Keep your eyes and ears open and always be prepared for opportunity. There are deals around every corner!

Mission Statement

Financial Freedom Through Foreclosures

To teach others how to successfully buy and sell property and increase their quality of life. The seeds you sow today will be the harvest you reap tomorrow!

Sharon's Story

I started in the real estate business at the age of 25. I was working for a large commercial investment company at that time and was watching it make millions. My husband did not want to work for others the rest of his life and was willing to do what it took to break away. He convinced me to give real estate investing a try, and we put our own home on the market. Our goal was to move into a fixer-upper, repair it, sell it, and do so over and over again while accumulating wealth.

My husband had to work hard to convince me to make this move, because I was raised by a father who was not a risk taker by any stretch of the imagination. He had brainwashed me to believe that your money was safe only in the bank, earning very little interest, and keeping your job for life was the wisest thing to do. Before my husband and I listed our home for sale to start investing in real estate for ourselves, I wanted to be perfectly prepared, so I decided I should get my real estate license, mortgage broker's license, and community association manager (CAM) license. I wanted to be safe! It turned out that the only license you need is your driver's license.

Four weeks after putting our home on the market, my husband was suddenly killed in a tragic accident. I was devastated and all my dreams were shattered. I had just lost the man I thought I would spend the rest of my life with. I was miserable. About six months later, I decided to pursue investing on my own and in his honor. I named my business after him and bought my first ugly house.

I hadn't quit my job yet because I was concerned about my income, but on the day I closed on my first deal, I was so elated I had taken that first step that I went back to the office and gave my two-hour notice—nothing that I recommend now, but I've never regretted it. I then made every mistake you could possibly think of on that house. I dove headfirst into investing and bought three other properties in my first year. I had those sold before I even finished my first deal—I almost became one of the desperate sellers we teach you to find. A few years later, I met Dwan and found that we had very similar goals and the drive to achieve them. After one year of successful business together, we became full-time partners.

A few years after that, we were asked to speak at a local real estate investment association. That was just the beginning. Folks were interested in learning how a two-woman team was succeeding, so we began to offer workshops, books, tapes, and more.

One of our transactions had us at the closing table unable to close because the property's payoff was more than anticipated. A phone call was made to the lender to ask for a delay or cancellation of the seller's foreclosure sale. Instead of postponing the foreclosure, the lender offered to grant us a short-sale. They faxed a new reduced payoff and we were able to close. This definitely intrigued us so we looked into it further, learning that most lenders were willing to do short-sales rather than foreclosures.

Our primary business was helping folks in foreclosure, so we began contacting lenders on every single transaction. As we began implementing this new strategy, we added more and more documentation to our offers, helping to make our case or justify the offer. We eventually organized an entire package that seemed to get us an acceptance letter nearly every time. As we spoke about short-sales with our fellow investors, we learned that they had no clue what a short-sale was when it came to real estate.

FIGURE I.2   Sharon and Hubby

Eventually, we were on the speaking/teaching circuit and traveling the country teaching only the short-sale technique.

We also co-founded the Florida Real Estate Investors Association, a monthly networking and continuing education organization dedicated to both aspiring and seasoned real estate investors.

Even though Dwan and I swore off dating other investors, I couldn't help myself. I married one! (See Figure I.2.) In addition to our other businesses, my husband, Juan, and I are very busy enjoying the life of full-time real estate investors, teachers, and mentors. I just gave birth to our first son, Joshua, and I truly enjoy the life and career I've chosen. This is what I was born to do and I love it.

My wish is for you to enjoy the same success and blessings we've been able to enjoy!

CHAPTER 1

Get Motivated, Set Goals, Get Started

Do you dream of financial freedom—having all of your bills paid? How about a beautiful second or third home? Does a cruise around the world seem appealing? If this sounds like the lifestyle you could get used to, we want to ask you a question: "What is stopping you?" We're serious! Why don't you have these things now? We ask this question each time we teach, but the answers are always the same:

"I don't have the education."

"I'm afraid of talking to homeowners."

"I don't know where to begin."

We have fantastic news for you—we're going to teach you how to overcome fear! We're going to teach you what to say to homeowners. We will teach you to be successful. We are going to teach you how to become a self-employed real estate investor and make more money than you ever imagined possible. All we ask is that you read this book and do what it says to do.

Real estate investing is a fantastic way for you to make an amazing living.

The benefits are incredible:

➤ Earning great money.

➤ Being your own boss.

➤ Controlling your own schedule.

➤ Making as much money as you want.

➤ Traveling to exotic locations.

➤ Sending your kids to the best schools.

➤ Taking care of older or ailing parents.

➤ Retiring early.

➤ Being able to shop without looking at price tags.

➤ Buying your dream car or boat or other toys.

➤ Living in a great house.

➤ Sleeping late on a Monday.

➤ Helping others while earning a great living.

➤ Working with those less fortunate than yourself.

One of our personal favorites is the wonderful feeling we get when we help homeowners out of a bleak situation. Watching them start their lives over with a newfound hope is a wonderful experience, and we're always thankful to be part of it.

When you conduct your business with a win-win attitude, business will follow you everywhere! You will be the investor whom everyone seeks out and wants to work with.

A Short-Sale Case Study—with a $200,000 Profit

Take a look at what this amazing business has done for Valerie Scott, from Baltimore:

Dear Dwan and Sharon:

When I purchased your course in late 2002, I had already been investing in real estate for several years. I thought I was doing quite well and had no idea of the impact your material would have on my life and investing career.

After glancing through the materials, I put them in a box in the basement to collect dust with my many other real estate books and materials. Then in March 2003, a friend who knew I was an investor approached me about purchasing her property. The property was a pre-foreclosure. I contacted her bank and they suggested I do a short-sale. I panicked. We were in the middle of a snowstorm, and I was unable to contact the few people I *thought could help me. I located the short-sale course among several boxes of books in my basement and quickly browsed through it. I followed the steps listed, using the scripts, letters, and examples as a step-by-step guide. I was able to negotiate a discounted payoff with the bank, locate a buyer, settle the property using a double closing, and make $25,000 on my very first short-sale deal.*

Now, approximately five years later, I am successfully doing short-sales in several states. My daughter, Daniela, joined my company two years ago. Our best short-sale in 2007 was a four-unit apartment building located in Washington, D.C. It was a referral from one of our local real estate investment associations. The property was owned by an investor whose real estate agent had unsuccessfully attempted to do a short-sale. Here is the loan information:

	Principal Balance	Arrears	Total Outstanding Balance	Short-Sale Amount Accepted
First mortgage	$655,479.79	$57,074.72	$712,554.51	$525,000.00
Second mortgage	$164,302.72	$16,193.81	$180,496.53	$10,000.00
Total	$819,782.51	$73,268.53	$893,051.04	$535,000.00

The mortgage balance was reduced by $358,051.04!

This deal proved to be quite challenging. Our biggest hurdle was convincing the mortgage companies that the value had drastically decreased, since the seller had owned the property for only a short period of time. Also, there were very few comparable properties in the immediate area that supported our offer. As discussed in your materials, Daniela was able to overcome this obstacle by focusing on the condition of the property as compared to other properties sold and by presenting local newspaper articles about the declining market conditions in the D.C. area. She also discussed how the property had previously been listed at market value but the real estate agent was unable to sell it.

Other major issues included holding the buyer until the short-sale was completed, along with title seasoning. Daniela continuously kept in touch with the buyer's agent. She provided an estimated short-sale time line and frequent status reports. Also, although we received multiple contracts on this property, we selected our buyer according to the seasoning requirements of the buyer's lender.

After two broker price opinions (BPOs), one appraisal, the buyer changing lenders twice, and using the "one more call to the lender" technique from "Short-Sale Secrets," Daniela was able to negotiate $358,051.04 off the outstanding balance owed to the seller's lenders, thus making the short-sale purchase price $535,000. We sold the property to the end buyer for $800,000 via a double closing. After all expenses, our net proceeds from this deal were $210,269.94! We purchased building materials for $10,000 from the seller, which he had previously brought to rehab the property. The seller was very thankful for our assistance and stated that prior to our involvement, this had been a trying and frustrating situation (see his e-mail letter thanking me, which follows).

We attribute our success to educating ourselves about preforeclosures and the short-sale process, which enables us to better serve our clients and community. We treat each homeowner with respect, care, and compassion. It is part of our mission to be a blessing to others as you have been a blessing to us. Thank you for providing us with the knowledge and tools needed to create financial wealth for our family and future generations.

Valerie Scott and Daniela Jones
Mortgage Debt Solutions LLC

Is that a great letter or what? Did you notice the paycheck? $210,269.94! If that doesn't get your attention, we don't know what will. The greatest part of this deal is that Valerie and Daniela helped a very distressed homeowner. In fact, the seller wrote them a thank-you letter, which they graciously allowed us to use in this book:

Dear Valerie and Daniela,

I just wanted to take the time to thank you for helping me sell my four-unit building in D.C. This was a very trying experience for me. By the time we met I was very frustrated. My property had been on the market for six months.

I was working with a Realtor who claimed she knew how to work a short-sale but at the same time was relying on me (someone who knew nothing about short-sales) for advice. After I contacted the local Real Estate Investors Association (REIA) groups, John P. put me in touch with you. That call was the best thing that ever happened to me. It was clear from the first conversation that Valerie understood my situation and knew how to proceed. Unlike the other Realtors I met who knew nothing about short-sales, Daniela was well informed and in turn kept me informed. I never felt like I was in the dark on the sale. Each document was explained to me until I understood what I was signing. Calls were always returned promptly. It took a few months to close, as you said, but it's over. The building has been sold and I can go about repairing my credit. Thank you for saving me from having a foreclosure on my credit report. Negative comments never seem to go away. Foreclosures can live for up to seven years on the credit report. I can't thank you enough for saving me from that. I appreciate all that you've done for me and would tell anyone facing the same situation to give you a call.

Thank you,

Stacey, a very distressed seller

Wow! What a great thank-you letter. If you ever wonder that you might be taking advantage of distressed sellers, keep this letter in mind. As you can plainly see, we are a true blessing for homeowners in trouble and offer a solid solution to a problem that sellers have no idea how to get out of. Are you beginning to see why we love this business so much?

Getting Motivated

So, what does it take to get started? *Motivation* is a great place to start! Motivation is the key to getting started. Many people only talk about doing something with their lives rather than taking action. We want you to actually do something with yours!

Starting something new is difficult for everyone. We know, because we were once where you are right now. However, we were more afraid *not* to try something new than to actually *do* something new. We knew that we did not want to continue the life we were leading.

- ➤ Working for people we didn't like.
- ➤ Having no real money to do anything.
- ➤ Being on a nine-to-five schedule.
- ➤ Having no vacations.
- ➤ Lacking a sense of accomplishment.
- ➤ Being told what to do all day long.
- ➤ Having no retirement in sight.

We believe that opportunity does not "knock," as many people say. Opportunity is around you all the time. It is up to you to recognize it. You have an amazing opportunity right now—to become financially free while helping people out of trouble. What will you do with this opportunity? Seize the day or let opportunity pass you by? We're betting you will seize the opportunity before you and change your life.

It is important to understand that deals are not found; they are made. You have to be willing to work and think outside the box. You must be creative when putting your deals together. Being creative in this business means structuring deals in a way that is often different from the way conventional real estate agents structure their transactions. By working creatively with homeowners, mortgage brokers, and real estate agents, you can put deals together that are outside the normal way of thinking (but are legal), and help more buyers get into homes they may not have been able to buy without your help and creativity.

We focus our business on people who are in distressed situations—divorce, loss of a job, a recent death in the family, increased mortgage payments due to an adjustable-rate mortgage, and much more. Because of this, most of our transactions are creative. Our goal is to create a win-win situation for everyone involved. If you help enough people get what they want, you'll get what you want, too.

Setting Goals

We really want to help you achieve your financial dreams and goals! However, to achieve a goal, you have to have one, and *it must be in writing*. Writing down goals is a big obstacle for some people. If this is the case for you, just ask yourself, "What is the worst thing that can happen?" The worst thing that can happen is that it will . . . come true!

Did you know that only 2 percent of people in the United States write down their goals? Isn't that shocking? Folks, without written goals, you won't succeed. We want you to be a superstar investor. As you become more successful, you can always change or modify your goals—in fact, *make them bigger!*

Without goals, you dramatically limit your success.

Include in your goals the specific steps that you are going to take to achieve them. For example, if your goal is to lose 15 pounds, how do you plan to do it? Write down the necessary steps:

> ➤ Go to the gym three times per week.
> ➤ Cut calories for all meals.
> ➤ Don't drink alcohol.
> ➤ Replace one meal with a weight-loss shake.
> ➤ Commit to doing this for 60 days!

This step-by-step process makes your goal realistic and attainable.

We want you to be a superstar!

Make sure your goals include the five equities of life:

1. Family.
2. Spiritual well-being.

3. Physical health.
4. Mental health.
5. Financial well-being.

The five equities of life are what make us who we are. It is important to keep balance with all of these:

> ➤ If your spiritual life is great, but your physical life is a mess—you will find it more difficult to reach your goals.
> ➤ If your financial life is great, but your family life is a mess—you won't enjoy the money.
> ➤ If you have old baggage hanging around—get rid of it today!
> ➤ If you are depressed over your lack of money—change your mind-set now.

We realize that doing this may be harder than it sounds; however, you *can* do it. You have to make the effort to have balance. It doesn't just happen. Schedule time for the gym, your children, church, spouses, and so on.

Strive to keep all areas of your life balanced.

Run your life as if it were a business, starting with one week at a time.

> ➤ **Monday**—walk for 15 minutes.
> ➤ **Tuesday**—attend a short moneymaking seminar.
> ➤ **Wednesday**—call your parents or family.
> ➤ **Thursday**—spend one hour reading a self-improvement book.
> ➤ **Friday**—take your kids to a movie.
> ➤ **Saturday**—walk for a half hour.
> ➤ **Sunday**—attend church.

Part of your daily goals should be to read and reread this book, and do what it recommends that you do. People fail because they try to do everything at one time. They decide to join the gym, quit smoking, diet, and spend time with family—all at the same time. They set themselves up for failure this way. Just make a small change each day. After 21 days, that small change will become a *habit*. After another 21 days, it will become a *lifestyle*.

We all have the same excuses for why we fail: We are too tired, we work too many hours, we can't fit anything else into our lifestyle and schedule. Folks, you are the *only* person holding yourself back. We know balance is tough when you are juggling so many things at once, but we have become masters at balance! We use schedules for everything from time with our families and friends to time off to relax. It is easy to do. Most of you schedule your day at work, but at night it becomes a free-for-all. *Organization is key to your success.*

We recently asked students at one of our boot camps how many of them wanted to make $100,000 or more this year. Every hand went up. Then we asked them how many had written goals and a plan to get there ... and most of the hands went down. Without a written plan, how do you possibly expect to become successful?

Here is an example: If you want to make $100,000 this year, you must plan to speak with X number of homeowners each month. Out of that number, you must plan to put together X number of deals. Out of those deals, you must plan to make X amount per deal.

If you put this in writing and stick to it, you will be able to achieve it. Why settle for $100,000 per year? There is no reason you cannot make a *million* dollars per year! We have many students who earn well over a million dollars each and every year. We want you to be one of them.

Millionaire Mind-Set

Write down your goals and look at them each day.
Measure yourself against your goals.
Keep track of what you have accomplished.
Treat real estate investing like a business, not a hobby.

Accomplishing Your Goals

It is a good idea to write down your goals on a piece of paper and keep a copy in a binder, as well as taping them to the bathroom mirror. This way, you will look at them daily. Sit down at the beginning of every week to see what you have accomplished, and then decide what needs to be moved to the next week. By keeping your goals in a binder, you can track how far you have come toward attaining your goals. We meet every week to discuss our goals from the previous week, to see what we have accomplished and to see where we need to focus our attention for the following week.

We each have weekly, monthly, and annual goals. Ninety percent of the time, we reach at least one goal that we write down. We write them down and read them daily.

This Is a Business, Not a Hobby

Whether you plan to invest part-time or full-time, take this very seriously. Use your time wisely and stick to a game plan. This is not a get-rich-quick business. You have to work smart, stay focused, and help people out to make money doing short-sale foreclosure investing.

One way you can work smarter is to set a daily schedule for yourself. If you know you have to call 10 people to get one appointment, or knock on five doors to see one homeowner, schedule your time so that you can accomplish these things—and stick to it!

If you are still working your full-time job, then schedule a set amount of time each evening to devote to this business. Maybe you set aside one hour per day and a few hours on Saturdays to do what is necessary to accomplish your weekly goals. When you set aside that time, be true to yourself and stay focused.

Start by seeing one homeowner each day on your way home from work. By seeing just five homeowners per week, that will be 20 per month, and that is 240 per year! With 240 homeowners under your belt, you can't help but make money! Even though it may seem as if you don't have a lot of time to devote to this business, you actually do. Likewise, if you are working full-time as a real estate investor, stay focused and stay on schedule.

Dealing with Naysayers

How do you keep a crab in a bucket? Put another one in with it. Seriously, one crab can climb out of a bucket, but two crabs can't. As one crab gets close to the top, the other crab grabs it and pulls it back down. Who, in your life, pulls you back down every time you try to get ahead? Come on ... we all have a crab in our bucket. Hey, wait a minute—*you're* not the crab, are you? Just kidding. You wouldn't be reading this book if you were.

Family and friends mean a lot to us, and their opinions can influence our decisions. You may even take their comments to heart and start believing what they say to you. Negative people say things like:

➤ You don't have a real estate license—how do you plan to be an investor?

➤ You don't have any money to do this business.

➤ You didn't go to college; what makes you think you can do this?

➤ What makes you think you will be successful when so many other realty agents and investors fail?

➤ You are a single parent—how do you expect to find time for this?

➤ You need to get your head out of the clouds and find a real job.

➤ You will fail, and then I'll have to say, "I told you so."

The people who care about you truly feel they are trying to help you avoid a bad situation. They convince you that you are being ridiculous for wanting to try something new, and their protest along with your inner self-doubt stop you from pursuing your goals and dreams. Don't listen to them or your inner voice. There is really no such thing as security anymore. How long will Social Security be available to Americans? How long before you are downsized? We all know how unreliable the term *job security* is.

We only believe we have security because we are not seeing behind the scenes. Does my boss *really* have enough money in the bank to cover my next paycheck? If so, for how long? Is management thinking of replacing me with someone younger and cheaper? If you rely on someone else for security, how secure is that? You need to be accountable for yourself and create your own job security.

Besides, do you really want to take advice from people who are making barely over minimum wage, telling you that you are ridiculous for trying to make it on your own? Or would you rather listen to someone who has ventured out herself, and has become successful? The answer to that question is easy. We both ventured way out of the box and became wealthy along the way. Our goal for you is to do the same thing. Won't it be great to be wealthy? Just think of all the great things you can do.

Personal Encouragement from Dwan

I have had many jobs I didn't like. In fact, I was fired from Denny's! As I was walking out of the building, I looked back at the Denny's sign and I remember thinking, "Who gets fired from Denny's?" It was a humbling day. Even after that, I continued to work for others. I did not have the confidence to venture out of my comfort zone . . . yet. Once my daughter was born, everything changed. My desire to give her a better life gave me the courage I needed to step out of the box and try it on my own. I encourage you to make the step now toward self-employment while things are good. Don't wait, like I did, until you are in a tough situation. It is a lot easier to be successful when you are thinking clearly and making a solid decision. If you are in a tough situation, then just suck it up and make the move—you'll find success just like I did.

Personal Appearance

In this business, it is important to be professional, but not intimidating. Pay attention to what your clothes communicate about you.

If you speak to distressed homeowners, a suit would be intimidating and would make it difficult to gain their trust. Wear a sport shirt with khaki pants or another casual outfit—something that portrays comfort. You want to be approachable and trustworthy, and always wear a smile!

Of course, there are times when you don't want to come across as too casual, either, such as when you speak with bank representatives or go to a closing. In this scenario, you want to be taken seriously and need to dress the part of the well-informed, successful investor.

Setting Up Your Office

When you first start out in this business, it is common to get overexcited and try to "buy the ranch before you know if the crop will grow," so to speak. Remember, when starting out, it is okay to keep your costs down by working from home and purchasing equipment as you close deals. Don't overextend your budget and end up scrambling to pay your bills. When this happens, you become as desperate as your sellers.

People need to be able to reach you in this business, and a *cell phone* is ideal. You can forward your home line to the cell phone, and therefore be accessible at all times. This is especially important when you run your ads, as it doesn't make sense to spend the money on advertising and not be reachable! When distressed homeowners finally get the courage to call, many times they will just hang up rather than leave a message if you don't answer right away. We can't stress this enough: *Be available!* One way to help determine which calls are coming in is to assign different ring tones for different callers such as "unknown" or "friends & family" or "business associates." This way you can effectively answer each incoming call.

It is not necessary to get a separate business line when starting out, as they are much more expensive than home lines or cell phones.

On the flip side of this coin, having a *dedicated fax line* is recommended when you start out, as it gives you more credibility with business associates. It also allows you the flexibility to conduct business at any time of the day or night. It may also be a good idea to have an 800 number for your dedicated fax line if you plan to conduct business in an area with multiple area codes, or handle out-of-state transactions.

There aren't very many people out there who don't know their way around a computer. This is another must-have when setting up your office. However, if you already own one, it is not necessary to go buy the newest model on the market. Besides, by the time you leave the store, it will already be outdated! Use your PC to create your own marketing materials in the beginning.

Remember, though, to promote your business at every meeting or event you attend. We even take it one step further—we speak with total strangers and promote our business that way as well. You never know when someone will know of someone else who needs help!

We have a line of clothing, Certified Investor Gear (www. certifiedinvestorgear.com), which we often wear. We have polo-type shirts, baseball caps, jogging suits, and more that state "I Buy Houses Cash" in bold letters. Every time we wear the clothing someone stops us to ask what the "I Buy Houses Cash" means. We get new students and deals galore just by making sure people know what we do.

We get testimonial letters all the time from students who have gotten deals at Blockbuster, at the car wash, and more. Make sure people know what you do. You walk past people all day long who could use your help, if only they knew you could help them. Become a walking billboard for your business.

Advertising pays!

Having a home office has definite benefits:

➤ Tax write-off.

➤ Convenience.

➤ Cost savings.

However, you may not want to use your home address as your business address for your marketing. We recommend retaining some privacy and utilizing a shipping office or post office box to receive your business correspondence. Another benefit to utilizing this option is that these stores typically will have a fax machine, and sometimes will provide administrative services as well.

Structuring Your Business

There are many ways to structure your business, including a sole proprietorship, an S corporation, a partnership, or a limited liability company. Consult a team expert (tax adviser or attorney) to help you decide which is best for you. There are different tax laws and legal implications with each, depending on the state you do business in.

There is a difference between an accountant and a tax adviser. An accountant is someone you meet with once a year to prepare your taxes, not to make adjustments to your business plan/structure. A tax adviser is someone you meet with throughout the year as you are earning income. The tax adviser can rearrange deductions based on your fluctuating income. It is important to understand your business goals when determining which entity is best for you and to relay your business plan to your adviser. This will better prepare you for year-end taxes and not surprise you with an unexpected expense due to the Internal Revenue Service.

If you are fortunate, you have found a tax adviser and an attorney who are versed in real estate practices. Meet with your adviser several times a year, and know that things will change as you progress. It is not necessary to know all the tax laws, but you want to work with someone who does!

Partnerships can be tricky. The old adage "Don't mix business with pleasure" is a strong statement. Regardless of your take on this saying, it is always wise to *put everything in writing*. If you choose the partnership route in your business, you will need a *partnership agreement*. Even if your partner is a family member or friend, or even your spouse, put all details of your intentions in writing. Everyone gets along great in the beginning when excitement is high, but not designating responsibilities can often break up a partnership. Discuss sharing the profits and the losses. No one ever anticipates losses when starting out, but you need to be prepared. If everything is in writing, you should make it through just fine.

Having a new partnership is a learning process. Not only are you learning the business, but you are also learning to work with one another, not to mention that the business will continually evolve over time. Learn your strengths and your partner's strengths, and determine which task is better for whom.

We consider ourselves lucky to have a partnership that has lasted over 15 years. We attribute our success to long talks, similar goals, and lots of meditation. With the right person, you could have a lifelong partnership as well. However, it is not necessary to have a partner to be successful. We both started out alone and did very well; we met, and decided to become partners after a year of doing deals together. Neither was looking for a partner. Once we got to know each other, we were smart enough to realize that if we put our heads together, we could make more money. That's exactly what happened!

Once you have determined the business entity that best fits your goals, you need to secure your business with a *bank account*. We highly recommend opening an account that is separate from your personal account, even if you are doing business in your own name or purchasing your first home. This method will make your record keeping much cleaner and keep your budget in line, as you will know exactly what your expense-to-income ratio is. This will also help you better determine your business plan and to see if you are on track with your business goals. Once you have opened your account, establish rapport with the bank representatives to prevent long holds on your deposited checks.

Ready to Do Business

No matter where you are, be prepared to do business at any time! Carry a satchel or briefcase with you that contains all the forms you will need should you run into a deal on the road. Other items you will want to have with you are:

> ➤ Blank contracts and other forms.
> ➤ Blue ink pens.
> ➤ A calculator.
> ➤ Business cards.

TIP: Do not to quit your full-time job until you are truly prepared for conducting business.

It is difficult not to get excited when a deal closes, but it may take you several months to find another one and close it. This is a fluctuating business that gets better as you gain experience, but newcomers should be patient in their desire to jump in with both feet. Don't be overzealous and end up in foreclosure yourself! If it took a month or two for a paycheck, do you have enough in reserve to fall back on? Get a few deals closed and build up a cash reserve, and then ... go for it! Investing should be fun, not stressful.

Your success depends on how smart you work. You have to keep yourself motivated and dedicated to doing this business or else there won't be an income. It is very easy to decide not to work a day for whatever reason, but that is one more day that won't bring in a paycheck. Don't waste your time during the week on nonproductive tasks, only to realize that it is the weekend and you haven't looked at any homes or spoken with any homeowners. It is very easy to get sidetracked when you don't have a boss breathing down your neck! You are your own boss now. Work like you would expect your best employees to.

Treat this adventure as a business . . . and it will treat you like a king or queen!

Being your own boss means that you have to be disciplined, be organized, and have written goals that you follow up with daily. Plan your day and stick to the plan. It is easy to decide to make calls the first two hours of the morning, but then start answering the phone instead and get sidetracked. Making those calls is what will get your foot in the door, so devote a certain time of day each day to do nothing but call homeowners.

What Is a Short-Sale? An Executive Summary of How to Negotiate with the Bank and the Homeowner

In a nutshell, a short-sale is negotiating with a mortgage holder to accept less than what is owed as payment in full.

A short-sale is our favorite investing strategy when we find a distressed homeowner who owes the bank close to or more than what the property is worth.

➤ Here's how it works: The homeowners owe $200,000 to their first mortgage holder and the payments are in arrears. Their property is worth $200,000 in retail condition. With the proper negotiating strategies, you get the bank to accept $100,000 as payment in full. Therefore, you are purchasing a $200,000 retail property for 50 percent of its value. Sweet, huh?

With proper negotiations you can take on deals that most investors pass up and turn them into amazing deals. Some of our largest checks have been from deals that had no equity.

There is a lot of controversy surrounding short-sales. Many investors state that banks don't do them or that you can't get good deals anymore. We have been doing short-sales since 1996, before we even knew they were called short-sales, and they are great!

The key to successful short-sales is to build a great case and a replicable business. When you get a short-sale accepted, do something nice for the bank representative. Take the time to build relationships within the banking industry. Building these relationships will help ensure your success. At some point, you'll be able to call the reps and simply make your offers verbally. Once the offers are accepted, the rep will tell you what to send.

Imagine only having to make a call and then, bam, the deal is done. Investors, that day will come. In the meantime, we'll teach you how to make money along the way.

Don't let anyone discourage you from becoming a short-sale expert. Do what we do, and you'll be very successful. That is what you want, isn't it?

Why Do I Need to Do a Short-Sale?

We are going to teach you the easiest way to make money investing in real estate: wholesaling properties (a technique we mentioned in the Introduction). There is one potential issue with wholesaling—properties with no equity. Today, many homeowners owe almost as much as their house is worth. When you find distressed homeowners willing to work with you and they have no equity, you can't wholesale the property. You must have equity to wholesale.

We are going to teach you how to *build in the equity*. Once you learn this technique, you will be unstoppable. Every phone call you get will now be a potential deal.

I had turned this particular seller down twice. No other investor would help him, either. He was overleveraged and going to foreclosure. Finally I made the deal work. I was able to help this person avoid foreclosure, help with his credit, and receive a $36,000 check, too! This was my first short-sale! Thank you, Dwan & Sharon!

Johnna Lodge, Georgia

Why Do Banks Accept Short-Sales?

There are many reasons why a bank will accept a short-sale. The main reason is because the payments are late and the homeowners can prove that they can no longer afford the property.

> ➤ The property does not have to be in foreclosure for the bank to accept a short-sale. Some banks require the foreclosure notice to be served, while others will accept a short-sale when just a few payments are late.

There is no specific number of payments that must be delinquent. Even one payment is enough at times. Often homeowners will call you when they are not yet in default, but cannot make any more payments. In this case, contact the bank, let them know that the homeowners will not be making any more payments, and open negotiations for a short-sale before the payments are even late.

Let's look at a few reasons why a bank might accept a short-sale:

> ➤ The mortgage payments are in arrears or foreclosure.
> ➤ The property is in poor condition.
> ➤ The homeowners have hardships and can no longer make the payments.
> ➤ New homes in the area are being chosen over existing homes.
> ➤ The area or neighborhood has depreciated in value.
> ➤ The bank's shareholders are concerned when there are too many defaulted loans on the books. Banks have reports due at the end of each quarter. They are more inclined to accept short-sales at the end of a quarter to clean up their books. The absolute best time to get short-sales accepted quickly is the last quarter of the year. We have called banks on December 10 and been told the short-sale would be accepted if we'd close by the end of the month! If you are reading this program in January, though, don't let that piece of information discourage you. Banks accept short-sales all year, but they do so faster in the last month.

➤ Some banks are required to prove a loss each month by writing off some bad loans; let's help them out.

➤ Some banks are required to keep a cash reserve of up to six times the retail value for *each* property they own, called **real estate owned (REO)**.

Real estate owned (REO)   Once a property is taken by the bank at a foreclosure sale, it is considered an REO. An REO is a liability for the bank, not an asset. Too many liabilities will cause any business to go under if not dealt with quickly.

It breaks down like this: The bank has a $200,000 property and is required to keep six times that amount as a cash reserve. This means the bank is sitting on $1,200,000 in unlendable money. (Imagine if the bank has 2,000 foreclosures across the nation!) The homeowner could drag the foreclosure on for two years utilizing the bankruptcy system. Would it be better for the bank to sit on $1,200,000 for two years or accept a short-sale today? The answer is obvious. The short-sale is a welcome relief.

➤ The area is crime-ridden.

➤ The area is riddled with foreclosures, proving a decline in the area.

➤ Many people don't realize that banks wholesale money. Banks borrow money from larger banks and lend it to you. These banks must show credit reports in order to borrow this money.

Every defaulted loan is like a black mark on the credit report. The more foreclosures a bank is carrying, the riskier it appears. If you were a larger bank lending to a smaller bank, would you lend your money to the bank with more or with less defaulted loans? Exactly . . . less! The smaller bank needs to borrow this money as inexpensively as possible so that it can make money lending it to you.

As you can see, a short-sale is often a welcome answer to a big problem. If the bank takes the short-sale, it can write off the loss and clean up the books before any reports are due.

How Much Do You Offer the Bank?

It is important to realize that when submitting a short-sale package, you are building a case. The better the case, the deeper your discount. As you read the rest of this book, you'll see that we focus on the case. Think of yourself as an attorney preparing for a court hearing. If the attorney shows up unprepared, the case will be lost.

How many of you remember the O. J. Simpson trial? If you think he was guilty, why do you think he walked away from a double murder charge? His attorneys built a great case, and it was presented more effectively than the prosecution's case was. Short-sales are the same concept: the better the case, the better the deal.

Having done so many short-sales over the years, we know exactly what the banks are looking for.

➤ Your first offer will focus on the homeowners, their distress, the distress of the property, and the overall hardship of the situation. This will be your initial offer and your lowest. You'll go up from there (and the bank will come down) until you reach a final settlement.

The best way to determine your offer is to first decide on your exit strategy. Let's use a $100,000 property with a $100,000 mortgage balance as our example.

➤ If you plan to wholesale the property to a rehabber, you need to know that rehabbers want to buy at no more than 65 percent of the retail value. This means that on a $100,000 property, a rehabber will pay up to $65,000.

➤ If you plan to rehab it yourself, you could pay as much as $65,000 or 65 percent of the value.

➤ Landlords will pay up to 80 percent of the retail value, or $80,000. When you find a property in mint condition, sell it to a landlord for a higher profit.

There are few things worse than making what you think is a good offer and the bank immediately says yes. Your first thought is that you are paying too much. We hate when that happens! We usually begin our negotiations with an offer of 40 percent of the retail, fixed-up value of the property. However, there are times we offer less and other times more.

Here are four examples:

> *Example 1:* Let's say the property is worth $100,000 in retail condition and the homeowners owe $100,000. Their property needs basic work: new carpet, updated kitchen and baths, and so on. On a property like that, we would start at 40 percent of the retail value, making our offer $40,000.

> *Example 2:* Let's say the same property needs $30,000 in rehabbing. Then we might offer somewhere between $25,000 and $30,000. Once the bank takes the property at the sheriff's sale, rehabs it, and pays the realty agent commission, it will make the same amount later as it will make selling it to you today.

> *Example 3:* This is the same deal as Example 1 with one adjustment. The property is worth $100,000 in retail condition as before, only this time the homeowners owe only $65,000. Again, the property needs basic work: carpet, paint, updated kitchens, and so on. Since the mortgage balance is $65,000, asking the bank to take $40,000 is not much of a short-sale. In this case, we might offer 50 percent of the mortgage balance, or $32,500.

> *Example 4:* The homeowners owe $100,000, but the property is in mint condition. We might offer as much as $65,000 or $70,000. We could sell it to a landlord for $80,000 and still have a great deal.

The bottom line is: There is no correct offer. The best way to determine your offer is to start with the *current* retail value and work backwards, depending on what your exit strategy is.

> If you plan to keep the property, you can offer more.

> If you plan to wholesale it (our main exit strategy still), you have to account for the rehabber as well as your sale proceeds.

> If you plan to sell it to a landlord, you can pay more.

For example:

Retail value	$100,000
Short-sale offer	$40,000

There is $60,000 left on the table. You plan to wholesale:

Rehab costs	$10,000
Cost of money	$5,000
Rehabber profit	$25,000
Your profit	$20,000

TIP: These techniques also work on commercial buildings, apartment buildings, and more.

This leaves a window to negotiate of $20,000. If the bank does not accept your offer of $40,000, you still have a $20,000 window. The more you pay, the less you make. The rehabber will still want to make $25,000, the cost of money will still be $5,000, and the rehab costs will still be $10,000. Your figure is the only number that is negotiable. If you raise your offer the entire $20,000, you will leave no money for yourself.

If you begin the negotiations at $40,000 and end at $50,000, you still make $10,000 for yourself—not a bad day's work.

Work the numbers backwards to determine your highest offer and start as low as possible. Having a larger negotiating window will allow you to get more of your offers accepted.

Here is a short-sale we recently did. This house was beautiful, which proves you *can* do short-sales of pretty houses. We did actually send the bank a complete short-sale package, but we just want to share with you the highlights of this great deal.

The seller of this new-construction home, which was absolutely gorgeous, had bought the home with $90,000 in down payment and builder extras. Since he owed approximately $483,000 (see Figure 2.1), which was what it was worth, we had to do a short-sale in order to create enough equity to make it worth purchasing.

FIGURE 2.1   Settlement Letter: Statement of Amounts Owed by the Distressed Homeowner Totaling $483,581.38

Law Offices of David J. Stern, P.A.

David J. Stern
Managing Attorney

Associate Attorneys
Miriam L. Mendiola
Samuel Hy Silverglate
Forrest G. McSurdy
Donna S. Click
Donna Evertz
Beverly A. McComas
Maria M. Solomon
Gregg R. Dreilinger
Mary Elizabeth Diaz
Wendy J. Wasserman
Stephen T. Cary
Robyn R. Katz
Alberto H. Hernandez

801 S. University Drive Suite 500
Plantation, FL 33324

Primary Phone (954)233-8000
Auto Attendant (954)233-8400
Primary/Foreclosure Fax (954)233-8333

Internet E-Mail dstern@dstern.com

Associate Attorneys
Billi K. Pollack
Lance E. Forman
Steve M. Binston
Frederic J. Di Spigna
Michelle K. Mason
Stacey D. Rosenthal
James Suglio
Sandra Ann Little
Damian A. Valladares
Sandra H. W. Hankin
Arthur J. Berk*
Neha Baumann*
*Of Counsel

*** CERTIFIED FUNDS ONLY ***
FUNDS MUST BE RECEIVED BY JUNE 23, 2006
THIS LETTER IS FOR SETTLEMENT PURPOSES ONLY.

JUNE 5, 2006

32 WEST REALTY, INC
FAX#: (561) 819-▬▬

RE: LOAN #: 001429▬▬
MORTGAGOR: ▬▬ ▬▬ ▬▬
PROPERTY ADDRESS: ▬▬▬▬▬▬▬ WEST PALM BEACH, FL 33413
OUR FILE: 06-▬▬ (EMC)

DEAR SIR/MADAM:

PURSUANT TO YOUR REQUEST FOR PAYOFF FIGURES AS TO THE ABOVE REFERENCED LOAN, THE FOLLOWING IS A BREAKDOWN OF THE SUMS CURRENTLY DUE AND OWING TO THE LENDER:

		PAYMENTS AND EXPENSES DUE TO LENDER:	$481,390.53
UNPAID PRINCIPAL BALANCE:	⋍$451,518.60		
INTEREST:	$ 24,073.49		
PROPERTY INSPECTIONS:	$ 15.90		
BPO	$ 100.00		
LATE CHARGES:	$ 368.26		
ESCROW TAXES/INSURANCE	$ 5,314.28		

		ATTORNEY FEES & COSTS DUE TO LENDER:	$ 2,190.85
TITLE SEARCH/EXAM:	$ 325.00		
TITLE UPDATE:	$ 75.00 EST.		
CLERK FILING FEE:	$ 267.60		
SERVICE OF PROCESS:	$ 315.00		
ATTORNEY FEES:	$ 1,200.00		
SERVICE/MAIL REQ'D BY LAW	$ 8.25		

TOTAL AMOUNT DUE: $483,581.38

During the short-sale process, the seller moved elsewhere (which is common). While the home was vacant, we began to market it. We began talking with the bank's loss mitigation department in June, and by the time the seller was able to gather all of the information we needed from him, we were ready to submit our short-sale package (see Figures 2.2 and 2.3). The $375,000 figure in Figure 2.3 represents the amount being offered to the bank.

In November, we finally received an approval at $347,168, which represented the net figure the bank was willing to accept

FIGURE 2.2   Payoff Note

PLEASE NOTE THAT FUNDS <u>MUST</u> BE TENDERED IN THE FORM OF <u>CASHIER'S CHECK OR MONEY ORDER</u> MADE PAYABLE TO THE LAW OFFICES OF DAVID J. STERN, P.A. TRUST ACCOUNT. <u>TRUST ACCOUNT AND ESCROW ACCOUNT CHECKS WILL NOT BE ACCEPTED UNDER ANY CIRCUMSTANCES</u>. THE FUNDS MUST BE RECEIVED IN OUR OFFICE NO LATER THAN THE CLOSE OF BUSINESS ON JUNE 23, 2006. FUNDS RECEIVED AFTER THIS DATE WILL NOT BE ACCEPTED.

ADDITIONALLY, YOU MUST CONTACT THIS OFFICE PRIOR TO TENDERING ANY FUNDS TO VERIFY THE TOTAL AMOUNT DUE. THE FORECLOSURE ACTION WILL CONTINUE UNTIL ALL FUNDS ARE RECEIVED AND ACCEPTED BY THIS OFFICE. ACCEPTANCE OF FUNDS IS SUBJECT TO FINAL APPROVAL BY OUR CLIENT. ALSO, PLEASE PROVIDE YOUR CORRECT CURRENT MAILING ADDRESS IN THE EVENT THERE IS AN OVERAGE AND YOU ARE DUE A REFUND.

NOTE: PLEASE BE ADVISED THAT THE SATISFACTION OF MORTGAGE WILL BE PROVIDED BY THE MORTGAGEE.

SHOULD YOU HAVE ANY QUESTIONS, OR REQUIRE ADDITIONAL INFORMATION, PLEASE DO NOT HESITATE TO CONTACT THIS OFFICE.

SINCERELY,

LEGAL ASSISTANT
REINSTATEMENT/PAYOFF DEPT.
EXT.193

*** CERTIFIED FUNDS ONLY ***

THE CREDITORS LAW FIRM IS ATTEMPTING TO COLLECT A DEBT FROM THE DEBTOR. ANY INFORMATION OBTAINED FROM THE DEBTOR WILL BE USED FOR THAT PURPOSE.

FIGURE 2.3   Loan Offer Fax Submitted to the Bank to Buy the House for $375,000

FAX COVER SHEET

32 West Realty, Inc.

32 S.W. 5th Avenue
Delray Beach, FL 33444
Phone Number: ▓▓▓▓▓▓
Fax Number: ▓▓▓▓▓▓

Send to: Chris ▓▓▓	From: Nicole ▓▓▓▓
RE: loan # 1002 ▓▓▓	Date: October 23, 2006
Phone number: 800-306-6059	Phone number:561-819-1900
Fax number: 720-241-7526	Fax number:561-819-5685

☑ Urgent   ☑ Reply ASAP   ☐ Please comment   ☐ Please review   ☐ For your information

Total pages, including cover: 12
Comments:

Chris,

Attached is an offer for $375,000 this is a great offer I hope you seriously consider the sellers have had the house listed since January of this year. We have received offers of $329k, $351k, $349k and $357k. the property is located inside a new community where the builder is selling larger homes and offering incentives that the Troung's can't even match given there situation. The house is small, one-story in a neighborhood of large 2-story homes and buyers are buying the new larger homes instead of high priced-used homes. I also attached the builders flyers with this fax with all the information on the other homes. Please contact me when you receive this fax. I look forward to your quick response.

I can be reached in the office at 561/▓▓▓▓ x 304 M-F, 9-5 est
Or by e-mail ▓▓▓▓▓▓
Thank you,
Nicole ▓▓▓▓

(see Figures 2.4 to 2.6). Because it was a large loan, the approval process took longer than usual. We were also delayed because the loan was sold, meaning that note investors purchased this loan from the lender as part of a package of defaulting loans; therefore, we

FIGURE 2.4 Specialized Loan Servicing Fax: Further Negotiations Lead to the Bank Accepting As Little As $347,168

Specialized Loan Servicing, LLC

November 30, 2006

<u>Sent via fax</u>

WEST PALM BEACH, FL 33413

Re: SLS Loan Number: ▓▓▓▓▓▓▓
       Property Address: ▓▓▓▓▓▓▓▓▓
                           L 33413

<u>Short Sale, Contingent Approval</u>

Dear ▓▓▓▓▓▓▓▓▓▓

Specialized Loan Servicing LLC (SLS) has been authorized by the Investor to accept a "Short Sale" in connection with the above-referenced property, contingent on the fulfillment of the conditions listed below:

1. Return of signed acknowledgement of the approval letter by fax.
2. Final HUD-1 Settlement Statement.

The above items must be received prior to closing in addition to the agreed upon proceeds as described below.

The minimum net proceeds approved of $ 347,168.00 must be received in our office before close of business on **12/29/06**. If you have not already done so, please send the requested documentation along with the name of the title company's closing agent and a contact number, so that we can make arrangements for direct payment of the proceeds to SLS. If any of the above requested documents and information as well as the minimum net proceeds are not received in this office by the dates given, this approval will be null and void and you will need to contact this office for updated approval.

You will <u>NOT</u> receive any proceeds at closing and will waive your rights to any unearned premiums for taxes and/or insurance and any escrow funds.

8742 Lucent Blvd., Suite 300, Highlands Ranch, Colorado 80129
Direct 1-800-306-6059   Fax (720)241-7526

FIGURE 2.5 Specialized Loan Servicing Fax, Page 2

Please be advised the acceptance of this short sale transaction is being made in reliance upon the information provided by you the debtor(s) in consideration for a short sale, including any and all financial representations regarding amounts and sources of income, other assets, and debt obligations of you the debtor(s).

At least 24 hours prior to closing, a copy of the final HUD-1 Settlement Statement must be faxed to the attention of the Customer Resolution Department for approval. If you become aware of any changes to the approved terms and the loan cannot close or fund, you should contact this office immediately.

All seller proceeds from the sale must be made payable to Specialized Loan Servicing LLC in the form of a Cashier's Check and remitted immediately after closing to Specialized Loan Servicing LLC, 8742 Lucent Blvd., Suite 300, Highlands Ranch, CO 80129. Proceeds may also be wired to:

- Bank Name   –   J.P. Morgan Chase Bank
- Bank Address   –   Houston, TX
- Account Number   –   0011-██████
- Bank ABA Number   –   021-000-021
- Account Name   –   SLS Wire Clearing

Please reference your name, SLS Loan number and property address for all payments. **After full completion of this document, please fax all pages to: 720-241-7526.**

Borrower's Day time telephone number: _____
                                   Mailing Address: _____
                                              City: _____
                                             State: _____
                                               ZIP: _____

My signature below acknowledges acceptance of the above terms and conditions.

_____
██████████████   **Date**

Sincerely,
SPECIALIZED LOAN SERVICING LLC
Customer Resolution Department
(800) 306-6059

8742 Lucent Blvd., Suite 300, Highlands Ranch, Colorado 80129
Direct 1-800-306-6059   Fax (720)241-7526

FIGURE 2.6 Settlement Statement

A. Settlement Statement

U.S. Department of Housing and Urban Development

OMB No. 2502-0265

B. Type of Loan

1.☐ FHA 2.☐ RHS 3.☒ Conv. Unins. 4.☐ VA 5.☐ Conv. Ins.	6. File Number 08-1049	7. Loan Number	8. Mortgage Insurance Case Number	

C. Note: This form is furnished to give you a statement of actual settlement costs. Amounts paid to and by the settlement agent are shown. Items marked "(p.o.c.)" were paid outside the closing; they are shown here for information purposes and are not included in the totals.

D. Name and Address of Borrower	E. Name and Address of Seller	F. Name and Address of Lender

G. Property Location	H. Settlement Agent
	TITLE RESULTS, INC. Telephone: (561) 498-8181, Fax: (561) 498-8801

	Place of Settlement 5300 WEST ATLANTIC AVENUE SUITE 404 DELRAY BEACH, FLORIDA 33484	I. Settlement Date 12/21/06

J. SUMMARY OF BORROWER'S TRANSACTION:		K. SUMMARY OF SELLER'S TRANSACTION:	
100. GROSS AMOUNT DUE FROM BORROWER		400. GROSS AMOUNT DUE TO SELLER	
101. Contract sales price	375,000.00	401. Contract sales price	375,000.00
102. Personal property		402. Personal property	
103. Settlement charges to borrower (line 1400)	27,240.12	403.	
104.		404.	
105.		405.	
Adjustments for items paid by seller in advance		Adjustments for items paid by seller in advance	
106. City/town taxes to		406. City/town taxes to	
107. County taxes to		407. County taxes to	
108. Assessments to		408. Assessments to	
109.		409.	
110. 2006 Real Estate Taxes	7,525.93	410.	
111. Capital Contribution	250.00	411.	
112. Maintenance Proration	48.39	412. Maintenance Proration	48.39
120. GROSS AMOUNT DUE FROM BORROWER	410,064.44	420. GROSS AMOUNT DUE TO SELLER	375,048.39
200. AMOUNTS PAID BY OR IN BEHALF OF BORROWER		500. REDUCTIONS IN AMOUNT TO SELLER	
201. Deposit or earnest money		501. Excess Deposit (see instructions)	
202. Principal amount of new loan(s)	355,000.00	502. Settlement charges to seller (line 1400)	18,241.09
203. Existing loan(s) taken subject to		503. Existing loan(s) taken subject to	
204.		504. Payoff of first mortgage loan	347,168.00
		Specialized Loan Serving, LLC	
205.		505. Payoff of second mortgage loan	
206.		506. Final Water Bill	150.00
207.		507. Maintenance Payment	1,620.00
208.		508. 2005 Real Estate Taxes	2,846.28
209.		509.	
Adjustments for items unpaid by seller		Adjustments for items unpaid by seller	
210. City/town taxes to		510. City/town taxes to	
211. County taxes to		511. County taxes to	
212. Assessments 01/01 to 12/21	7,299.12	512. Assessments 01/01 to 12/21	7,299.12
213.		513.	
214.		514.	
215.		515.	
216.		516.	
217.		517.	
218.		518.	
219.		519.	
220. TOTAL PAID BY / FOR BORROWER	362,299.12	520. TOTAL REDUCTION AMOUNT DUE SELLER	377,324.49
300. CASH AT SETTLEMENT FROM OR TO BORROWER		600. CASH AT SETTLEMENT TO OR FROM SELLER	
301. Gross amount due from borrower (line 120)	410,064.44	601. Gross amount due to seller (line 420)	375,048.39
302. Less amounts paid by/for borrower (line 220)	362,299.12	602. Less reduction amount due to seller (line 520)	377,324.49
303. CASH FROM BORROWER	47,765.32	603. CASH FROM SELLER	2,276.10

SUBSTITUTE FORM 1099 SELLER STATEMENT: The information contained herein is important tax information and is being furnished to the Internal Revenue Service. If you are required to file a return, a negligence penalty or other sanction will be imposed on you if this item is required to be reported and the IRS determines that it has not been reported. The Contract Sales Price described on Line 401 above constitutes the Gross Proceeds of this transaction.

SELLER INSTRUCTIONS: To determine if you have to report the sale or exchange of your primary residence on your tax return, see the Schedule D (Form 1040) instructions. If the real estate was not your primary residence, complete the applicable parts of Form 4797, Form 6252, and /or Schedule D (Form 1040).

You are required by law to provide the settlement agent with your correct taxpayer identification number. If you do not provide your correct taxpayer identification number, you may be subject to civil or criminal penalties imposed by law. Under penalties of perjury, I certify that the number shown on this statement is my correct taxpayer identification number.

TIN#

12-21-2006 at 3:55 PM

RESPA, HB 4305.2 - REV. HUD1(3/86)

had to wait until the new owner/lender assigned their loss mitigation representative to this short-sale; hence the delay between the payoff statement and our offers being submitted.

In the meantime, an interested buyer made an offer but couldn't produce proof of funds, so we dismissed him. He continued to call, expressing how much he wanted the house and asking for more time to find the money to close. We really didn't give him much thought. Another interested buyer went to the property and told us that it looked occupied. To our surprise, the buyer who had been calling had actually broken in and moved in. He painted, decorated, and filled it with his furniture! Once we found out, we imposed rent and forced a closing deadline or else we would have to take some legal action.

He closed before our short-sale approval deadline, and everything worked out fine! We have to say that this was a first. We'd never before had an interested buyer move in ahead of the closing. The great news is that the deal worked out for everyone, creating yet another win-win situation.

The bank accepted over a $100,000 discount! Do not be afraid to make a low offer. The worst-case scenario is that the bank says no.

The Biggest Mistake New Investors Make Is Offering Too Much

If your offer does not embarrass you, it is too high! You can always go up ... rarely down. Do not be afraid to make low offers. The worst that can happen to you is that the bank will say no, and then you will make a higher offer. A rejection is not the end of the world, so offer low. We can't stress enough how vital this is to your success.

We want to make a point here. Regardless of the property value, start your offers at 40 percent. We are using an example of a $100,000 property. You may live in an area where the average property sells for $500,000 or $2 million or more. The value of the property has little to do with the offer. Actually, more expensive properties can be easier to short-sale because of the cash reserve issue. The cash reserve is the amount of money the bank has to keep aside (cannot lend out) for each REO it has in inventory. For some banks, it's two times the value of the property; for others, it's much more. This really ties their hands—after all, a bank's business is lending money.

Successful Short-Sales Start with the Homeowner

Let's say you've already completed step one—you have found an interested homeowner couple. Once you have determined that they have no equity, explain the short-sale concept to them and let them know that if you are successful in your negotiations, you'll be able to help.

➤ Be certain they understand that if you cannot come to an agreement with their bank you will not be able to help them and they will still be in foreclosure.

You must negotiate the following with the homeowners before you proceed with your end of the deal:

➤ The amount of money they will receive for moving expenses.

➤ The homeowners' move-out date.

I found a distressed property and sold it to an investor for a $59,000 profit! I still can't believe it. I made what used to be my full year's salary in one transaction! It took only about six days, from start to finish, to find the homeowners and do the paperwork and that sort of thing. It took 30 days to close on the transaction. In that short amount of time, I made all that money! I owe a lot of thanks to Dwan and Sharon for helping make this all possible.

Dave Mitchell, Georgia

Financial Agreement with the Homeowners

➤ When dealing with homeowners without equity, we explain that one of their best solutions is a short-sale.

➤ We explain to the homeowners that if we can negotiate with their bank to accept less than what is owed as payment in full (as long as the amount is acceptable to us), we will purchase the property.

➤ We also explain that we need their help in obtaining the short-sale, as the bank will require items that only they can provide.

If they are in agreement, then we proceed with executing the paperwork for our short-sale package.

➤ One of the first questions you should ask the sellers is what they are seeking as a result of your help.

The answers will vary from "Nothing—just help my credit" or "Three thousand dollars to get moved with" to an unreasonable amount of money that will kill the deal.

Most homeowners with no equity simply want out of their situation. We always tell them that if we are able to work out a deal with the bank and actually purchase the home, we will give them whatever they need to move with.

There are two reasons for this:

1. We want to help them financially.
2. If the sellers should move out during the short-sale negotiation, we want to maintain communication with them in case the bank requires additional information.

Knowing that they will receive cash when the deal is complete will motivate them to continue to cooperate with you.

Any amount of money you agree to give the homeowners is fine; however, this figure cannot appear on the closing statement. It must be on a separate agreement. We use a bill of sale because it is a legal way to provide financial assistance to them. Typically, one of the bank's conditions for accepting your short-sale is that the sellers do not receive any sale proceeds. The bank will not accept thousands of dollars less than what is owed by the sellers, pay all the sellers' closing costs, and then allow the sellers to leave the closing with a profit. Can you blame the bank for that?

➤ The legal way to avoid this problem is to pay the sellers to clean the house or for another service, such as debris removal.
➤ You can also buy appliances, computers, baseball cards, antiques, furniture, cars, or anything else of value via a Bill of Sale.

When purchasing an item from them, you are legally *buying* something, not giving sale proceeds.

To do this, you must use a bill of sale (see Figure 2.7).

FIGURE 2.7 Sample Bill of Sale (Downloadable*)

Known all men by these presents that _____

(Buyer), in the county of _____, in the state of

_____, for TEN DOLLARS AND OTHER GOOD AND

VALUABLE CONSIDERATION, paid _____ (Seller) in

the county of _____, in the state of _____, the

receipt of which is hereby acknowledged, has bargained and sold the following

property and/or goods:

_____

For a value of: _____

_____   _____
Buyer   Date

_____   _____
Seller   Date

In witness whereof, the Seller has executed this Bill of Sale this _____

day of _____, in the year _____.

Notary Public: _____ Commission expires: _____

*Copyright © 2008 by Dwan Bent-Twyford and Sharon Restrepo. To download and customize this form for your personal use, please visit www.theieu.com/shortsaleform.

When possible, we buy items that have a perceived value. If we pay the homeowners $5,000 for a baseball card collection, who is to say what it is worth? If you are an avid collector, it might be worth even more to you. Your reasonable opinion dictates the price. There are baseball cards that sell for $100,000 each, but there must actually be a baseball card collection you're buying of course.

How Much Should You Pay the Homeowner to Move?

What is a fair amount of money to give homeowners in foreclosure? There is no real answer. We feel that they should not be rewarded for failing to make their mortgage payments; however, they do need to move and start over.

There are many gurus teaching investors to give the homeowners $500 and tell them to move out.

Here is our question to you: Can you move with $500?

If not, why would you expect someone else to? These homeowners are trying to start over. They need money for a moving truck; for their first and last month's rent, as well as a security deposit; and for deposits for electric, gas, water, and phone service, to name a few of the expenses they face.

Be fair when dealing with these folks. You have 20 deals around the corner, but this is their one and only chance to start fresh. Remember what we always say: You reap what you sow, so sow some good seeds.

Setting the Move-Out Date

Here is the key question we use to encourage homeowners to move out quickly:

"When are you planning to move in with family?"

Without being blunt or rude, this question will imply that they must move out soon and will put the thought in their minds that they could move in with family. Most homeowners aren't thinking clearly and don't consider that as a possibility until we mention it.

Moving in with family is a great option. There will be no requirement for a credit check or for first and last month's rent and security deposit (money they don't have and would want from you).

It is impossible to expect the sellers to move out immediately when you are not promising an exact result. When they are not moving in with family, they often need moving money. Therefore, they will remain in the home until closing.

How do you handle homeowners who need to stay in the property until the day of closing?

➤ Hire a moving truck the day of closing.

➤ Have the movers load the homeowners' belongings.

➤ Have the homeowners come to the closing while the moving truck is in the driveway of the subject property.

➤ Before and after the closing, go to the property and do a walk-through.

➤ Determine if the property is in the same condition as when you went to contract.

➤ Buy something from them and give them the cash so they can get going.

➤ Pay the movers yourself as a good deed.

Why should the homeowners be out by the closing?

➤ If you have wholesaled the property to a rehabber, the rehabber will want to begin work immediately.

➤ If you give them several days to move out and they don't, guess what? Your rehabber now has to go through the eviction process (not a good way to build a relationship).

➤ One of the homeowners could get into a car accident or die before they move out. Your rehabber now has to evict a widow or widower or put someone out who is now disabled or recuperating.

➤ The homeowners could file for bankruptcy and live free in the rehabber's property for months.

➤ The homeowners could fall asleep smoking in bed and burn the house to the ground.

➤ A natural disaster could come along and destroy the property.

Why do any of these things matter to you? Because you are trying to build a replicable business. If you have sold the property to rehabbers and now the rehabbers can't get the homeowners out, they will never do business with you again.

In addition, if you plan to keep the property for a rental or to rehab it yourself, you now have a major problem that could become very costly.

You *never* want homeowners living in a house you are either buying or selling, just in case. One wrong move and you are in a lawsuit.

I found a property that broke down like this:

Amount owed: $165,449

Short-sale price: $100,000

Sold for: $180,000

Appraised for: $210,000

This was an amazing deal. Thanks!

David J., Maryland

CHAPTER 3

Expert Strategies for Finding Distressed Properties and Foreclosures

New investors often worry that there will be too much competition for short-sale foreclosures, but we are here to tell you that there will always be distressed home-owners, for whatever reason, who need your help! There are millions of foreclosures each year in the United States. There is also an equal number of divorces, bankruptcies, probate situations, layoffs, relocations, and illnesses. The list is endless. We try to buy directly from the distressed homeowners when possible, because it saves them from a final foreclosure on their credit report; however, don't overlook the hundreds of thousands of bank-owned properties. The banks are inundated with foreclosures and will be for years to come.

Here are our favorite and most profitable ways to find great deals.

Buying Bank-Owned Properties for Pennies on the Dollar

As we said, we prefer to deal directly with distressed homeowners; however, banks have great deals, too. One of the team players you will need in order to buy bank-owned properties is a real estate agent. This agent will play an important part in your success.

The easiest way to find an investor-friendly real estate agent is to attend your local Real Estate Investors Association (REIA) group.

Another method is to contact the real estate owned (REO) departments of major banks and ask the reps where they send their foreclosures once they take the properties at the sheriff's sale. The rep will give you the local real estate office that lists the bank's foreclosures. Go to that office in person and meet the agents. These agents work with the banks, foreclosures, and, most likely, investors.

Our agent searches the Multiple Listing Service (MLS) constantly looking for deals using key words like:

➤ Handy.

➤ Fire damage.

➤ Foreclosure.

➤ Tender loving care (TLC).

➤ Bank-owned.

These words usually mean there was some type of distress and the bank now owns the property. Since banks are in the business of lending money and not owning properties, they are receptive to selling these properties below market price.

When we make a low offer to the bank, we like to justify it.

➤ Let's say the bank is asking $85,000 on a property worth $100,000. We usually offer 50 percent of the retail value. In this case, we'd offer $50,000.

Will you get some of these low offers? Believe it or not, yes! We average at least one deal a month from our agent.

The agent prepares the offer, and we include:

➤ Pictures of the damage to the property.

➤ Low-priced comparable properties (comps).

➤ A cover letter stating why we are offering less than market price.

➤ Articles from the newspaper showing problems with the neighborhood.

➤ A cash offer.

➤ Closing in 30 days.

➤ No inspection period.

Do these items help? We think so. Banks are in the business of lending money. Having a number of defaulted properties on their books does not make them look good in the eyes of their shareholders. The banks are as anxious to get rid of these properties as you are to buy them.

Due to the fact that the banks don't like assignment fees, you'll need to double close—covered later in the book.

We also make our offers without requiring an inspection period. The bank gives us one anyway to avoid a lawsuit later should the property have a major problem. The bank typically gives seven to 10 days for inspections. We make cash offers, do not require inspections, and state that we will close quickly so the bank will take our offers seriously.

If the property is in decent shape, other investors will make offers as well. The stronger your offer, the better your chances for a yes from the bank.

Figure 3.1 shows a sample cover letter to the bank.

As you can see, this is a simple letter. We want to bring it to the bank's attention that the property is distressed and that we are making a serious offer.

When you buy properties directly from the bank, you cannot use a $10 deposit as you can with an individual homeowner. Banks usually want at least $1,000 with the initial offer. The bank will give you seven to 10 days for inspections. Read the inspection clause carefully to ensure that your deposit will be refunded for any unsatisfactory inspection obtained by you that would cause you to cancel the contract. At the end of the inspection period, if you plan to stay in the deal, a larger deposit will be due. During the inspection period, you will find a rehabber, get the property under a second contract, collect a large deposit from the rehabber, and then use that deposit for the bank, making sure that your second contract discloses this fact.

If you are unable to find a rehabber during the inspection period, simply tell the bank you have decided not to purchase the property. The contract will be cancelled based on unsatisfactory inspections and the bank will give back your $1,000 deposit.

Being a new investor, you may want to complete a few deals with homeowners before you move on to bank-owned properties. The banks are easy to deal with, but if you don't close (after the inspection period expires, for any reason), they will keep your

FIGURE 3.1   Sample Letter of Intent (Downloadable*)

Dear Mr. Banker:

Upon my inspection of [address], I find that the property needs a lot of work to bring it up to current market standards. I called a real estate agent in the area and requested the current market values. I have based my offer on the market values as well as the necessary repairs.

I am offering [amount] cash, closing in [amount of time], and asking for no inspection period. Based on the area comps and the amount of damage to the property, you can see that my offer is more than fair.

I have enclosed pictures as well as articles from the local papers. As you can see, the house and area are distressed. I am willing to purchase the property, but I must be able to buy it right. I don't want to lose money.

Please review the attached documents and respond at your earliest convenience. I urge you to accept my proposal and move for a quick closing on this property.

Thank you for your cooperation. I look forward to working with you.

Sincerely,

[Your name]

*Copyright © 2008 by Dwan Bent-Twyford and Sharon Restrepo. To download and customize this form for your personal use, please visit www.theieu.com/shortsaleform.

deposit. That means that if you put up a $1,000 deposit and can't find a rehabber, your deposit is history.

Likewise, if you use the rehabber's deposit and the rehabber doesn't close, the rehabber's deposit is history, as well. In this case, the bank keeps the deposit. If you took a $3,000 deposit from the rehabber and then gave $1,000 to the bank, you'd still have $2,000. If the rehabber doesn't close for any reason, the bank would keep the $1,000 and you would keep the $2,000. Remember, the only way the bank can keep the deposit is if either you or the rehabber doesn't close. If the bank can't close, everyone gets their deposits back.

Banks are great to deal with. Be sure you find a real estate agent as soon as possible.

If buying directly from the banks interests you, read on.

Newspaper Ads

This is an excellent way to entice people to call you. We run our ads under the Real Estate Wanted section.

Here are some samples:

Distressed? Overwhelmed by bill collectors?
Facing Foreclosure? I can help. 555-555-5555

WANTED!! Distressed properties.
Confidential telephone consultation. 555-555-5555

Cash for your house! Any condition—any situation.
No equity, no problem! 555-555-5555

Be prepared. When you run these ads, your phone will ring off the hook! Make sure the greeting announcement on your phone mentions the ads that you have running so callers know they have called the right place. You may have one ad running for distressed sellers and another running to build your buyers list, so make sure that your announcement is generic.

Here is a sample greeting for you:

"If you are calling about the newspaper ad, please leave your name and number. Your call is very important to me, and I will get back with you shortly."

Respond to messages as soon as you can, as time is of the essence. People who call because of your ads are probably responding to other investors' ads as well. It takes courage for distressed homeowners to reach out for help. If you are able, visit the homeowners the same day you get the call and try to negotiate a deal before another investor gets the deal. Situations will vary, so legally be the intermediary putting buyers and sellers together, and earn a lucrative living doing it!

"I Buy Houses for Cash" Street Signs

"Cash for Your House" street signs have been an incredible success for us. The first day we used these signs, we had received six calls by the time we'd put out only 25 signs! Another day we put out 13 signs and wrote three deals by the end of the day. We earned over $85,000 on those three deals! The trick is to keep the signs simple—don't get wordy. Two lines should cover it—one for the message and one for your number. Make both lines large and easy to read from a moving vehicle. You can purchase these signs for a little as $1.50 each in boxes of 100 from a marketing company or over the Internet. If you are on a tight budget, these signs are a great place to start! Attach the signs to wooden stakes and place them on exit ramps, street corners, and median strips.

However, some areas have covenants that don't allow these signs to be posted, so check with your county or municipality for restrictions or requirements or to obtain a permit. Use common sense when putting up your signs and you should avoid law enforcement asking you to take them down. Another great place to put them is in the yard of your own rehab properties. Any rehabber would love to have more houses to work on in the same neighborhood.

Networking

The world is full of opportunity, and it is up to you to take advantage of that opportunity. We are always networking with people, no matter where we are. We leave business cards at the dry cleaners, in restaurants, at the gym, at school, and so on. Other great places to network are through your church, charities you participate in, or groups you belong to. Let everyone know that the next time they run into someone needing help, you are available to do just that! Again, don't forget to actively participate with your local Real Estate Investors Association (REIA). Visit www.flreia.com to see an example of the one we operate in Florida to find out how a REIA can benefit you in your area.

Postcards

We have had tremendous success through mailing out postcards over the years. We mail to everyone in the public record—foreclosure, divorce, bankruptcy, behind on taxes, and landlords. Distress comes in many forms. For example, a couple who jointly qualified for a mortgage are now divorcing and one is left to struggle with trying to make the payments. By mailing to people going through divorce, you may be able to help them avoid foreclosure before it becomes an issue. The same goes for bankruptcy—we already know that these people are struggling. By contacting them now, you may be able to work with them before they get into foreclosure.

Once again, all this information is available at your local courthouse, but you can also subscribe to a service that provides this information. Some companies provide mailing lists that can be purchased. Title companies can also obtain mailing lists. When sending out postcards, though, remember to put "or current resident" after the addressee's name. This way the card will not come back to you, but will go to whoever lives in the home currently. We all know that life can change in the blink of an eye. Someone may not need your help today, but if you continue to farm the same area, you may end up being that person's lifesaver later on.

When sending out postcards, keep your theme focused on solving problems rather than offering cash for homes. Homeowners are often looking for other preferable solutions, although they realize that they may have to sell their home.

Magnetic Vehicle Signs

The nice thing about magnetic vehicle signs is that you are always working. Whether you are driving or parked, people have access to your phone number. People use these signs because they work. A set of signs can cost about $50 from a sign shop. Prices will vary depending on where you purchase the signs. Keep your messages simple and easy to read. The bigger the sign, the easier it will be to read and remember. Some investors may worry that this is tacky, but after getting a check for $25,000 as a result of your vehicle sign, your attitude will definitely change!

Bail Bondsmen

You're probably thinking, "What? Why would anyone call someone like that for real estate deals?" When someone gets arrested, what happens to them, besides going to jail? Right, a bail bondsman often gets them out. What does the bondsman often take for collateral? Yes, deeds to properties. You would be stunned how many properties you can get from a bail bondsman.

➤ A bondsman would much rather have the cash than the property. When you get a call, negotiate the best deal you can and get the deed.

You can find bondsmen in the Yellow Pages. In most cities their offices are near the courthouse. Take a day to go to the county courthouse and stop in as many offices as you can find. Meet the owners in person, let them know what you do, leave a card, and see what happens.

Several states don't offer the bond service when someone is arrested. You should be able to find this out about your state simply by opening the Yellow Pages.

We did a class over the phone recently (we called it a "teleboot-camp"; see www.theieu.com), and meeting bondsmen was part of the homework we assigned the class. Several of our students had deals in the first week. One student secured five deals from one bondsman. Be like these students—make the effort and see what happens.

Pawnshops

Pawnshops are another highly overlooked method of finding properties. People sell all sorts of items at pawnshops to get quick cash:

➤ Jewelry.
➤ Lawn equipment.

➤ Television sets.

➤ DVD players.

➤ Guns.

➤ Coins.

The pawnshop gives you cash for the item, and you get a ticket. The ticket gives you a certain amount of time to redeem the item or make a payment. If the payment is not made on time or the item is not redeemed, the pawnshop keeps the item.

The larger pawnshops often have:

➤ Cars.

➤ Boats.

➤ Houses.

➤ Airplanes.

Look in the Yellow Pages or take a drive one day and stop by a few pawnshops. Ask if you can put a "I Buy Houses for Cash" sign with no phone number in the window. Tell the pawnbroker that when anyone inquires about the sign, if he will get the person's name and number you'll make the contact.

When you close a deal, the pawnshop owner will want to be paid an advertising fee for putting your sign in the window. If the pawnbroker gives you the name and number, he has a way to follow up on the deal to make sure you're not cutting him out. Once you have done a few deals and trust has been established, you can use a sign with your contact information.

The bail bondsmen may let you place a sign in their windows as well.

Always be creative when looking for deals. Take a look at what Mark did:

Dear Dwan and Sharon:

One of the most rewarding short-sales I ever did was a deal I had in West Palm Beach, Florida, about three years ago. I have known Sharon and Dwan for the past eight years and have not only taken their boot camp on short-sales, but also partnered with them on several deals. Their knowledge in short-sales is what led me to be so successful in the market.

A homeowner contacted me, saying he just wanted to get rid of his home (or "headache," as he called it). He owed almost as much as it was worth at the time. Although it did have some equity, the homeowner didn't want to bother with trying to get the property ready to market and sell. He had two mortgages on the property and also had a lien attached by a creditor. His first mortgage holder had issued a foreclosure against the property and the homeowner wanted out. He had a new job and fiancée waiting for him out of state. I offered him $300 in exchange for the deed to the property. He took the offer and signed the house over to me.

I immediately started negotiating with the lenders and the lien holder. Since I had a copy of the lis pendens issued from the first mortgage holder, I used that as leverage. First up was the lien holder. I called him and let him know his lien of $2,300 was about to be wiped out at the courthouse when the property went to foreclosure sale. I offered to settle the debt in full for $400. He countered with $1,500, and I countered back with a final offer of $500. Needless to say, he took it. Step one was complete—I had just settled a $2,300 lien for $500.

My next target was the second mortgage holder. The second mortgage balance was $40,000. I used the same approach. I gave them a copy of the lis pendens and told them I was buying the first mortgage and continuing with the foreclosure. They were made aware that if I took the property to foreclosure sale, their mortgage of $40,000 would be wiped out and they would receive nothing. My first offer to them was $500. We went back and forth a half dozen times with offers and counteroffers. They finally settled their $40,000 note for $10,000. Step two was complete.

Now was the tough part, the first mortgage holder. I knew this would be the biggest challenge, but I had a strategy. An addition to the back of the house was begun but never completed. There was *exposed electrical and plumbing work. I took some unflattering pictures as well as letting the lender know that code enforcement had been out to the house and was threatening to slap the house with violations. This was enough to make the lender flinch and agree to discount the mortgage by $17,000. Now, between the first and second mortgage, in addition to the lien holder, I had created almost $50,000 in additional equity!*

I did the limited amount of rehab needed on the property and put it up for sale. Since the house was bigger than almost every other house in the neighborhood, I was able to get top dollar for it. When all was said and done, I walked away with over $43,000 in profit! I have you two, Dwan and Sharon, to thank for teaching me the skills to help get the lenders to discount the mortgages through short-sales. It has changed the way I'm able to do business as an investor.

Thank you,
Mark Lopez

Isn't that another great deal? A profit of $43,000. The best part is that another homeowner was helped and had a chance to get a fresh start. Let's look at a few more ways to find sellers in distress.

More Deal-Finding Favorites

Whether you put "I Buy Houses for Cash" signs in the windows, pass out flyers, give business cards, or hang a banner, these are more fantastic places to search for your next deal:

➤ Advertise on billboards.
➤ Advertise on bus benches.
➤ Call charities and places that help families in distress.
➤ Call churches—did you know that people often leave their prop-
   erties to their church when they die?
➤ Meet mail carriers—they see vacant properties every day.

➤ Meet the utility meter readers—again, vacant properties.

➤ Call the local fire department—they know when homeowners have been displaced by a fire.

➤ Contact the police—they can tell you about vacant properties as well as properties that have been vandalized.

➤ Meet the guy who shuts off the water.

Other places to consider for signs and ads are:

➤ Buy here, pay here car lots.

➤ Mom-and-pop convenience stores—most convenience store chains like 7-Eleven won't allow you to post ads, as they are corporate owned and usually can't get permission.

➤ Mom-and-pop grocery stores.

➤ Check-cashing stores.

➤ Antique stores.

➤ Indoor flea markets.

➤ Outdoor flea markets.

➤ Doctors' offices.

➤ Dentists' offices.

➤ Gyms.

➤ Restaurants—eat-in and take-out.

➤ Anyplace that is owner operated.

Offer an advertising fee to anyone who agrees to help. Ask your attorney how to legally pay them so that you can account for the money.

CHAPTER 4

How to Approach the Homeowners and Create a Win-Win Solution

We believe and the Bible states that we reap what we sow. If you conduct your business without integrity, you will have to pay the consequences. If you take advantage of homeowners in distress by not doing what is best for them, you will find yourself at risk of a similar circumstance. If you treat homeowners with respect and understanding, you will receive respect in return. This is true for everything in your life—not just investing. "Do as I say *and* do as I do." Practice what you say you will do, and be an example for others to admire.

Distressed sellers can be anyone; they are abundant because there are many reasons for their distress:

➤ Foreclosure.

➤ Bankruptcy.

➤ Divorce.

➤ Job relocation.

➤ Owner of two homes unable to afford both mortgages.

➤ Failed relationship and painful memories with the home.

➤ Inheritance where the inheritor can't afford the tax or payments.

➤ Stock market fluctuation.

➤ Landlords tired of having tenants.

➤ Increased mortgage payments from adjustable-rate mortgages.

Whatever the situation, a motivated seller is a homeowner you can talk to and possibly help through some creativity that other realty agents or investors may not have thought of.

Distressed homeowners have a desire to explain their situation to you—they don't want you to judge them or think that they are losers because of the situation they are in. Honestly, a distressed situation can happen to anyone! Life throws a loop in your routine, and before you know it you are behind on payments for your home. Suddenly you find yourself in the worst situation you can imagine, and are facing the loss of your home. Homeowners have a great deal of pride, as most of us do. If you are compassionate and take the time to listen to homeowners, you will do well in this business. If you have been in a similar situation, let them know that you fully understand how they feel and what they are going through. It helps them feel more comfortable if they know you truly understand.

So listening to the homeowners' story is the first step. You will not only understand their situation, but you will become aware of the level of their motivation. This will save you time as you progress as an investor. We have learned that we want to spend time only with homeowners who are truly motivated to get out of their situation. Sometimes the homeowners aren't ready when you first approach them. We let them know that we are available when they have made the decision to get out of their distressed situation, but until they are truly motivated to do as we direct them to, we need to work with others who are motivated *now*. You can't afford to waste your time on people who just aren't ready to listen to you and do what it will take for them to get out of their situation.

Understanding Why Homeowners Want to Work with You

Word of mouth goes a long way when trying to build your business. If you create win-win solutions, you will certainly be the person who is referred to by friends, family, and even strangers as deals arise. It takes understanding the mind-set of the homeowner, good ethical practices, and willingness to go above and beyond the call of duty for the homeowner. Many investors have given this business a bad reputation due to their unethical practices. Don't become one of those investors! It feels good to know that you made a difference in homeowners' lives, and have given them a chance that they may not otherwise have had.

Understanding what motivates sellers will help you determine your process for meeting their needs. You cannot convince someone to be motivated. First, you have to find out what their motivation is for selling their property and what they want out of the deal. We teach our students to ask, "What are you seeking as a result of my help?" If the homeowners need money or a car, or want to move closer to their relatives, they will tell you. They may simply need help repairing their credit. Listening to your homeowners will not only show them that you care, but it will help you understand their motivation behind their situation.

Consider this scenario: The homeowners say they need $10,000. We ask them why they need that specific amount. They then say that they need a car. We network with many people, including car dealers, and if we can get them a car for $4,000 instead of $10,000, we have just met their need and saved ourselves $6,000! They have the car they need, and we have the property.

When homeowners ask us, "What will you give me for my house?" our answer is always the same: "What is it that you are looking for that we might be able to help provide?" Then we can work toward a win-win situation for all of us.

Building Courage to Knock on Doors

"Knocking on doors" doesn't mean you have to physically go from door to door with no leads. Start with public records and find out who is in foreclosure and then knock on the doors of people from that list. Still, knocking on doors is one of the oldest and best techniques for obtaining deals. Why? Because others hate to do it! Investors' greatest fear with knocking on doors is not knowing what to say. They also are afraid the homeowners will slam the door in their faces. If that happens, so what? Move on to the next deal. Obviously, we expect you to use caution when using this incredibly bold technique. Remember the three key words in investing:

Motivation, motivation, motivation!

You may need to make several offers before the first one is accepted. However, that one yes will be more than worth it! With more experience, you will get more offers accepted. With more experience, you will also overcome the objections that homeowners and banks may throw at you. There have been a few times when we have received several days' worth of no's; however, we continued knocking on doors, and eventually found someone who really needed our help—and that made it all worthwhile.

Keep your script simple when knocking on doors. Many times the homeowners will give you a preprogrammed "No, thanks" or "I took care of it" because they don't want to explain their situation or want anyone else to know about it. However, the blank look on their faces when you ask what they did to take care of it speaks volumes. Be creative, but sympathetic to their situation. A no is not a definite no in most cases.

Friendly Negotiations with the Homeowners—What to Say and What You Need from Them

Here is a script to get you started:

YOU:	Hi, Mr./Mrs. Smith. My name is Jane, and I was at the courthouse doing some research. I noticed that you have a pending problem with your property. I specialize in helping folks like you solve their problems, and I was wondering what I can do to help you.
HOMEOWNER:	I took care of it.
YOU:	You took care of it. Great! What did you do?
HOMEOWNER:	I hired an attorney.
YOU:	You hired an attorney—good move! What did your attorney advise you to do?
HOMEOWNER:	He told me to file bankruptcy.
YOU:	Bankruptcy. Interesting. Did you know that once the bankruptcy is dismissed, you will still have a foreclosure on your record?
HOMEOWNER:	No, I didn't know that.

YOU: As I mentioned, I specialize in helping folks like you, and can offer you several solutions that will buy you more time in your home. Shall I come in and explain those options to you now, or come back at six o'clock when your spouse is home?

HOMEOWNER: Let's do six o'clock.

It is that easy! You will find that the more you practice your scripts and objection handlers, the easier your conversations will become, and the more fluent and unrehearsed they will seem. It is like learning a second language—it takes practice, but it is not that difficult to do.

As you may have noticed, we repeat the homeowner's answers. This gives them positive affirmation and lets them know that we are listening to them. This is called "repeat, approve, and respond" or cause-and-effect language. This type of repeating brings familiarity into the conversation and builds rapport with the homeowner.

➤ *By repeating homeowners' words*, we not only sound familiar to them, but they feel that we are listening, and this causes them to instantly bond with us.

➤ *By giving a positive response*, we help homeowners feel as though they have made a good decision. In a troubled time, that is a welcome feeling.

➤ *By asking questions*, we steer the conversation in the direction we want it to take and maintain control.

This method of speaking is an entire learning process in itself, called *neurolinguistic programming*. It is an art of persuasion and can really make a difference in the number of deals you complete each year. Just by repeating, approving, and responding, you will close more deals than you thought possible.

Here are some dos and don'ts when you knock on doors or meet a homeowner in person:

➤ Do not wear sunglasses. Homeowners can't see your eyes and you will seem like a suspicious person.

➤ Never wear a hat with a visor, like a baseball cap. Again, if homeowners can't see your eyes, you will seem suspicious.

➤ Always have a clipboard in your hands so that both of your hands are visible. If you tend to stand with your hands in your pockets or behind you, the homeowners will be wondering whether you have a weapon and are going to rob or kill them and will not hear what you are saying.

➤ Never wear cologne or perfume. We know this one seems strange, but let's look at it from the homeowner's point of view. You're a guy and you wear Eternity. You show up at the door and a woman answers. Her husband used to wear Eternity. He ran off with another woman and she still hates him for it. You are wearing what the ex-husband used to wear, and sub-consciously you remind her of him so she now dislikes you. The same goes for the girls, too. You don't want to remind the homeowners of someone they now dislike.

➤ Be aware of the color of your clothing. Green promotes trust, while red promotes dominance. We like warm or quiet colors like green, blue, pink, or brown. Stay away from reds and blacks.

➤ Dress casually, but professionally—no suits. Also, lose the jewelry. Homeowners losing their home do not need to see that you own a Rolex.

➤ Be aware of what you are driving. If you ordinarily drive a Rolls-Royce, you may want to consider getting a middle-of-the-road car for meeting homeowners. Yes, homeowners need to see that you are successful to feel confident that you can help them. No, they do not need to see that you have become a millionaire from distressed properties. You never want them to wonder if you have taken advantage of others and that is why you have so much stuff. People are leery to begin with; don't feed into it.

➤ Be certain you are speaking to the right person. Instead of blurting out why you are there, ask if this is Mrs. or Mr. so-and-so first. Once you are sure, continue with your conversation.

➤ Never use the "f" word..."foreclosure." State that you were doing some research and see that they have a "pending problem with their property," and that you would like to help them. This puts the blame on the property, not the person.

Establishing Rapport over the Phone

Speak at the same rate of speed as the homeowners. For example, if the person who answers the phone speaks slowly, do the same. If they speak fast, do the same. People who speak fast think that people who speak slowly are dumb. Likewise, people who speak slowly think that fast talkers are slick and untrustworthy. Is it true? No, it is a subconscious thought that most people are not aware of. When you follow the homeowner's rate of speech, you seem familiar and the homeowner likes you without necessarily knowing why.

Ask them to share a little about their current situation, and listen with respect and empathy. Once you feel that they have properly vented, begin to ask for details about their situation. Homeowners want to tell you what happened, because they don't want you to think that they are losers. No one grows up with the goal of being in foreclosure. Something in their lives changed, and they want to be certain you know what it is.

Make an appointment to view the property, and then call back to confirm the appointment. During the second phone call, ask more questions. Be certain that everyone on the deed is home and willing to put a deal together.

When on the phone, listen for the objections you are going to get when you meet in person (for example, "We don't have to sign a deed, do we?"). If they ask questions on the phone, be ready to handle them in person.

Knock on Doors Like a Pro

Something else to consider when meeting homeowners face-to-face is your safety. We have knocked on doors alone many times. That was probably not the best way to do it, but it never occurred to us that something bad might happen to either of us. Even though we never felt as if we might put ourselves in danger, we did carry Mace. You never know when you'll get a flat tire in a rough neighborhood or get the feeling of impending danger. Use your common sense and you'll be fine.

When knocking on doors,

- ➤ Two girls can go.
- ➤ A guy and a girl can go.
- ➤ A guy alone is okay.
- ➤ Two guys is a no-no.

If two girls knock on a door and a woman answers, she will most likely feel safe because they are all girls. If a man answers, he is likely to feel embarrassed that a woman is trying to help him out of financial trouble. Traditionally men are supposed to be the breadwinners. He will still work with two women, but it may take a few minutes to establish rapport.

If a girl goes with a guy, it shouldn't make much difference whether a man or a woman answers. If a woman answers, the girl should speak. If a man answers, the guy should speak. Safety shouldn't be an issue, because the woman will feel safe because another woman is there.

If a guy goes alone and a woman answers, as long as he keeps his distance from the door, she will probably feel okay. He must keep his hands visible at all times. If a man answers, the two guys will bond.

If two guys go together and a woman answers the door, she may be thinking they are there to rob or kill her, not to help her. She'll feel overwhelmed by two strange men at her door and will not hear a word they say. If you are a two-man team, one can knock on the door, while one waits in the car. Once rapport is established, ask permission to bring your partner to the door. If a man answers, however, it will be no big deal.

One last tip before we move on: When homeowners state that they "have taken care of it," we like to ask if they are using the "loopholes in the foreclosure system" to extend their time in their property.

Nine out of 10 times, they'll ask, "What loopholes?"

We say, "No one has shared any of the loopholes in the fore-closure process? You're kidding! Do you mind if we come in and discuss some of your options?"

We realize that right now you are thinking, "Dwan and Sharon, I don't know any loopholes or options. Why would I say that?"

You could:

➤ Work out a loan modification with the bank on their behalf.

➤ Work out a forbearance agreement with the bank on their behalf.

➤ Take the property "subject to."

➤ Help them do a deed in lieu of foreclosure.

➤ Refer them to a bankruptcy attorney to discuss Chapter 13 bankruptcy.

We realize that right now you may not know many of these options, but we'll cover those next. Our goal is to help the seller the best way possible, and people love the word *loopholes*. The great thing about these options is that they may help the homeowners stay in their house longer. Sadly, once the foreclosure process is over, the bank takes the house at the sheriff's sale, and the homeowners are kicked out of their home.

Helping Homeowners Understand Their Options

Most homeowners believe that their only option is to lose their home to the foreclosure process. Often, they don't realize they can still sell their house, modify the loan, or even file bankruptcy to extend their time. Our job is to share the options the homeowners have and help them pick the option that is best for them. Although we would like to buy the property, if that is not the best option for them, we don't push for it.

They may be better off staying in their home and getting their payments back on track. We can't tell you how many times we have helped homeowners *for free*. For example, in one case the best option was a repayment plan, so we called the bank on the homeowners' behalf, worked out a deal for them, and went on our way, charging them nothing. Remember what we said earlier: You reap what you sow. For every freebie you do, there will be many profitable deals down the road.

Again, we always have another deal around the corner; this is the homeowners' one chance to get a fresh start. Learn the different options and help them make a sound decision.

Loan Modification

When a homeowner gives us a chance to explain their options, we start by explaining a loan modification. The loan modification simply means to change or modify their original loan.

For example:

Value of home	$200,000
Amount owed	$185,000
Monthly payment	$1,500
Payments behind	10
Back payments owed	$15,000
Attorney fees	$2,500

On behalf of the homeowners, you call the bank and explain that the homeowners have saved up enough money for several payments—let's say five payments for the sake of this example. Explain that the homeowners want to modify their loan. You want the bank to accept the five saved payments and put the other five late payments, plus any fees, on the back of the loan. This will increase the length of the original loan by a few months. Instead of a 360-month loan (30 years), the homeowners now have a 365-month loan.

Typically, the bank will require 50 percent of the late payments, plus any attorney fees, to do a loan modification. If the homeowners have not saved any of the money that was supposed to be used for mortgage payments, you would not be able to take advantage of this option. We typically start with this option because it is the simplest solution. Unfortunately, most homeowners have not saved any money, so we then need to move them mentally to a more realistic option before they lose their house to the foreclosure process.

Some homeowners do actually save some money. They are under the impression that they must have *all* the money before the bank will speak with them. Even though the homeowners are getting mail from the bank, they typically aren't opening it. If they did, they'd see that they could call the bank and do this option themselves.

TIP: Currently, homeowners are entitled to four loan modifications over the life of their loan. However, they can do only one per year.

If the homeowners have late payment fees, unpaid real estate taxes, property inspection charges, or forced insurance that has been added to their mortgage balance, the bank will most likely expect this money as well.

Once the loan modification is completed, the homeowners are completely out of foreclosure. If they miss any more payments, the bank has to start the foreclosure process over from the beginning. Because of this, the bank wants to make absolutely sure the homeowners can make the payments again. If the homeowners are out of work or have not resolved what caused the foreclosure to be initiated, the bank will not do a loan modification.

Forbearance Agreement

A forbearance agreement is a fancy word for a payment plan. The main difference between a loan modification and a forbearance agreement is that the homeowners remain in a state of foreclosure during a forbearance agreement.

For example:

Monthly payment	$1,500
Payments behind	10
Attorney fees	$2,500
Total due to bank	$17,500

You call the bank on behalf of the homeowners, just like a loan modification. The bank agrees to accept half of the money owed and will take the other half over the next 24 months. During this 24-month repayment plan, the homeowners are still in foreclosure, but the bank does not move forward with the process. They are at the same place in the foreclosure process as they were when the payments restarted.

With a forbearance agreement, the late payments are added onto the original payments until the last payment is made.

For example:

The original payments are $1,500 per month.

The bank is owed $17,500 in late payments.

The homeowners pay half now—$8,750.

This leaves a late payment balance of $8,750.

Divided into 24 payments, the late payments equal $365 per month.

The $365 late payment is added to the original payment of $1,500, totaling $1,865.

For the next 24 months, $1,865 is the new payment.

At the end of 24 months, the payment goes back to the original payment of $1,500 per month.

Why would the bank do a forbearance agreement instead of a loan modification? Everyone qualifies for a forbearance agreement. We've never come across a bank that won't at least give the homeowners a chance to repay their loan. Even if the bankers feel that the homeowners really can't repay their loan, they agree to a forbearance so that the homeowners are still in a pending state of foreclosure. This way, the bank can take the property faster, if necessary.

Sadly, most homeowners are unsuccessful in the forbearance agreement and end up right back where they started. Like a loan modification, if the homeowners have saved no money, this is not an option, either.

Subject To

"Subject to" means that the homeowners deed you their property subject to the existing loan. We take houses "subject to" often. It is a great way to collect rentals. The homeowners qualified for the original loan, their names are on the mortgage, and they deed the house to you. Now you have a property you did not have to qualify for. All you have to do is make up the back payments and keep the payments current for the life of the loan.

We make an agreement with the homeowners to pay the late payments and bring the mortgage current, and to continue to make the monthly mortgage payments until the property is sold or we refinance it. Before we part with any of our own money, we file the deed at the courthouse to protect our interest. Once the deed is filed, we are now the owners. We then give the homeowners moving money, make up the late payments, and find a tenant.

Typically we agree with the homeowners to refinance the property or sell it within three to five years, and at that time, their names will no longer be on the mortgage. By us making the payments on time, we are helping to reestablish the homeowners' poor credit. Once the mortgage payments have been made on time for several years, it is easier for the homeowners to buy another house or car.

By now, you must be wondering why a homeowner would choose this option. The homeowners don't know us from Adam, yet they are willing to deed us their property while their names are on the mortgage. When homeowners find themselves in foreclosure, they often "just want out" from underneath the property; they don't care how it happens. They trust you will do as you stated and make their payments on time.

The downside of a "subject to" for a homeowner is that the investor may make the mortgage payments late, or not at all, making the homeowners' bad credit worse than it already is. As an investor, our goal is always to help the sellers, not hurt them. Even so, once in a while investors get in over their heads and can't continue to make the on-time payments anymore.

➤ Should you find yourself in this unfortunate situation, you could do several things: For example, try to sell the property to another investor to take over the payments from you, or contact the sellers and see if they want the house back or know anyone who wants it from you.

If none of these options work, the property would end up back in foreclosure. If you got a good enough deal, you should never be faced with this situation. Fortunately, we have never defaulted on a "subject to" property. It is very unlikely that you would, either, but it is possible. Our suggestion is for you to wholesale as many properties as you can until you have cash and a very firm grasp on investing. We don't want to take over one of your properties.

We have many rentals that we have gotten in a "subject to" situation. In all cases, we refinanced or sold the properties within five years and took the homeowners' names off the mortgage. It was win-win for all of us.

Before you consider a "subject to," make sure it is allowed in your state. Some states are instituting predator laws to protect homeowners from investors who are trying to take advantage of them. Sadly, a few bad seeds ruin it for the rest of us. One of the many techniques predators use is to take the deed to a distressed homeowners' property with the understanding that the homeowners can stay in their property, file the deed, and then kick the homeowners out. The homeowners gave away their ownership when they signed the deed over to the predators, so they have no leg to stand on.

A few homeowners have called district attorneys and complained, and that is why the new laws are in place: to protect innocent homeowners who believe the investors. It is difficult for distressed homeowners to know whom to trust when they are in such a bad situation to begin with.

TIP: Put the name of the district attorney on the back of your business card and say to the homeowners, "If I don't do everything I say I will, you can call the district attorney and turn me in."

With that bold approach, I can't imagine a homeowner not wanting to work with you.

Deed in Lieu of Foreclosure

Banks will sometimes ask the homeowners to deed the house to the bank in lieu of going through the foreclosure process. This is a great option for the bank, but not for the homeowners. It saves the bank the expense of having to foreclose, but the homeowners typically end up with a foreclosure on their credit report.

The bank represents it to the homeowners as an "easy, friendly" foreclosure. The reality is that the bank may still pursue the homeowners for money if the bank does not break-even or make a profit when it eventually sells the property. In most cases, the bank will put a foreclosure on the homeowners' credit report, even though the homeowners never actually went through the foreclosure process. It can be a win for the bank and a loss for the homeowners.

We have come across many homeowners on the verge of deeding their house back to the bank. Thankfully, we came along and explained what was truly about to happen. The only way a deed in lieu of foreclosure is a good plan for the homeowners is if the bank will put in writing that it will not put a foreclosure on the homeowners' credit report and will not pursue a deficiency judgment if the bank loses money once the property is sold.

If homeowners can get both those promises in writing, and their attorney reviews this option with them, then a deed in lieu is not a bad option. If not, then the homeowners are much better off working out something with you.

Chapter 13 Bankruptcy

Only a bankruptcy attorney can be used for this option. A Chapter 13 bankruptcy is the reorganization of debt. A Chapter 13 will stop the sale of the homeowners' property. If homeowners call you close to the sale date of their property, there is not much you can do. If they want to file bankruptcy to extend the litigation process, which buys time, you can attempt a short-sale after they have filed bankruptcy.

Final Thoughts

Once we have exhausted all of the options homeowners have, we ask what they'd like to do. Most do not have the money for a forbearance or loan modification, they don't usually want to deed the property back to the bank, and most don't want to file bankruptcy, so we are left with a "subject to" or a short-sale. Of course, we choose a short-sale so we can wholesale it for a quick profit.

If we come across a property we'd really like to keep for a rental, we pursue the "subject to" option. As we have said and will continue to say, we do what is best for the homeowners. We always have another deal around the corner; this is their only chance to get a fresh start. Make sure they walk away with a good impression of investors. Our livelihood depends on it.

We are going to close this chapter with a success story from one of our students. Just look at the great results you can expect when you put the homeowners first.

Dear Dwan and Sharon:

I would love to share some of our short-sale highlights with you. Our very first short-sale deal came about when my business partner, John, was standing in line at the counter of the auto repair shop. A fellow in front of him was explaining to the mechanic how he had lost his employment and his house was now in foreclosure. John simply asked if he knew all of the options available to him to stop his foreclosure and stay in his home. The guy was very interested, and he became our first short-sale client. Even though we purchase a foreclosure list for nine counties each week, you never know where your next client will come from. It could be the auto repair shop!

When we spoke to our client's lender, we used your scripts to give us the confidence to call and a place to start. The loss mitigation department is always so busy at every bank. Having patience is the best asset that anyone can have. Right away I learned that I was going to spend some time on hold. I also learned that I would usually get the loss mitigation representative's voice mail and need to leave a message, and wait for them to call me back at their convenience. I called the loss mitigation representative on our first short-sale every day for one week, with no call back. After a week, I found out that the representative was on a week-long vacation and she had failed to tell me that she would not be available. She was slightly embarrassed and she was actually much easier to deal with after that. She must have felt really awful. All I can say is that patience is a virtue when negotiating with any bank.

We wholesaled our first deal and sold the property to a rehabber-investor at the same time—a double closing. We closed first with the bank, and then we closed with the wholesale buyers. We found our closing agent at our local Real Estate Investors Association (REIA) group, and they handled our double closing with ease. They are the experts and work with investors all the time. Finding a title company that not only knows how to do a double closing but does a lot of them each month is a must.

We left the closing with a profit of $35,000 and a very big smile on our faces!

Almost every seller that we have ever dealt with has been very happy and some even thrilled. Our first client was no exception. We stopped his foreclosure, we got the bank to waive any deficiency judgment, and after everything was completed, we bought the storage shed in his backyard for $2,000. It gave us a chance to provide him with some much-needed money.

By the way, a year and a half later, this client called us. He explained that he was back to work at his previous employment, he was making good money, and he wanted to know if we could help him buy another home. Now that is what we consider a win-win.

We did make one big fat mistake on our first short-sale deal. Let me preface this by saying that we had a conversation with Dwan at one of Dwan and Sharon's seminars that John and I attended. Dwan warned us to make sure that we had complete control of our deal and everything involved in it. She also suggested that we use all of our own contacts for closing. We did not listen closely enough, because we set our closing date for three days before the foreclosure sale date of the property, and let the buyer use his own mortgage company. Needless to say, the day of closing came and the buyer's money was not available. The next day, the buyer's mortgage company was still unsure *and needed more time. On the third day at 10:00 A.M., we were facing losing the deal the next day. We finally went to our bank, pulled out $96,000, and closed on the property. Two hours later, our wholesale buyer's money did come through, and we sold the property for a $35,000 profit.* We will never cut it that close again!

Over the past few years, we have completed two or three short-sales each year. This year, with the help of five partners who are now working with us, we are looking to close 12. Our goal is one per month.

Thanks,
Randy Holden

CHAPTER 5

Preparing Your First Offer

You've found a property and home-owners who want to work with you. Now, let's talk about the items needed to submit your offer to the bank—your short-sale package. We'll outline the basic steps to a successful short-sale and then walk you through each step in detail.

1. Find a property owner in distress.

2. Put a deal together with the homeowner.

3. Have the homeowner sign an "Authorization to Release Information" form.

4. Fill out a sales contract for the amount you want to offer the bank, and have the homeowner sign it.

5. Call the loss mitigation department at the bank.

6. Fax the bank your offer, along with the following:

   ➤ Your cover letter explaining why you can't offer full price and asking for a waiver of deficiency.

   ➤ The sales contract.

   ➤ Justifying comparable properties (comps) of the area.

   ➤ Pictures, if you have them.

   ➤ A net sheet or closing statement, also known as a HUD-1 (this shows the bank exactly how much it will net after closing costs, taxes, and so on are paid).

   ➤ A hardship letter from the homeowner that mentions the dreaded word *bankruptcy*.

   ➤ Estimated list and cost of repairs, using retail repair prices that the normal homeowner would pay for these items.

Before we go through the step-by-step short-sale process, we want to share Pete's story with you. If this doesn't motivate you, we don't know what will.

Dear Dwan and Sharon,

It is with great pleasure that I am writing this letter as a testimonial to the expertise and prowess of Dwan Bent-Twyford and her foreclosure and short-sale programs.

My wife, Pamela Thomas, and I studied real estate investing for four whole years before buying our first investment property in August 2004. We would probably still be studying if we had not come across the materials offered by Dwan and her business partner Sharon. As a direct result of purchasing and implementing their materials, we were able to generate wealth and regain our health. Let me explain.

In the spring of 2005 I was selected to appear on NBC's hit reality show The Biggest Loser. *But to go on the show I would have to drop everything, travel to California, and live in seclusion on the Biggest Loser Ranch. I would receive no pay for my participation on the show—contestants would have to make it financially the best way that they could. My wife Pamela and I knew what we would make through our newly acquired knowledge of foreclosures.*

Through lots and lots of hard work I was able to succeed with my weight-loss goals, as I lost 185 pounds in nine months in 2005. We were also able to succeed financially through the knowledge we gained from Dwan's programs.

You see, while I was away working out four hours each day on the Biggest Loser Ranch in California, Dwan was having a foreclosure boot camp in downtown Detroit. My wife was there. That summer Sharon came to Oakland County for an all-day Saturday foreclosure seminar. We both were there.

Dwan's method of doing foreclosures the old-fashioned way through knocking on doors is what directly led to us being in a financial position to basically be able to take off a year and regain our health.

Here are a few deals that we directly ascribe to Dwan's old-fashioned methods.

Ann Arbor, Michigan—Our first short-sale in 2005 was a Federal Housing Administration (FHA) property (when others told us you could not do a short-sale on an FHA property); we purchased it at 10 A.M. and sold it at 2 P.M. the same day for a tidy $20,000 profit.

Fernwood, Ann Arbor, Michigan—This was a two-bedroom condominium appraised at $140,000. Our purchase price was $35,000. We still own it and rent it out today.

Ailsa Craig, Ann Arbor, Michigan—This was a four-bedroom home appraised at $240,000. Our purchase price was $140,000. We still own it and rent it out today.

And there are others as well.

The single best way for us to thrive in the unique real estate market of Michigan is by purchasing properties at steep discounts. This has meant that we have had to purchase these properties for as little as possible through personal interaction with the homeowners. These methods are what we learned from Dwan's programs.

Last year we started our own business doing short-sales for Realtors and other real estate investors, and this spring (May 2008) we are scheduled to teach a class on foreclosures at Washtenaw Community College here in Ann Arbor, Michigan.

It is with great vigor that we highly recommend the foreclosure programs and strategies of Dwan Bent-Twyford and Sharon Restrepo.

> *Sincerely,*
> *Pete and Pamela Thomas*
> *Gideon Investment Group LLC*
> *info@gideoncompanies.com*

FIGURE 5.1 Pete Before and After

Pete also enclosed a before and after picture (see Figure 5.1).

Wow! We don't think Pete is the Biggest Loser; we think he is the Biggest Winner. What a story. He is such an inspiration.

We had intended to include one of our successful short-sales here to show you an actual deal, but after getting Pete's testimonial, we decided to include one of his. It would be easy for us to include one of ours; you expect us to have plenty and for them to be good deals. We feel that by seeing what students are doing, it helps you realize that you, too, can be a success in every aspect of life.

The paperwork from just one of the many deals Pete and his wife, Pam, have done is shown in Figures 5.2 to 5.16. This property had a mortgage balance of approximately $119,000. They were able to get the bank to accept $72,000. They rehabbed it and sold it for $139,000. This was a win-win for everyone. Pete even included a picture of his rehab. This was a fun and profitable deal for Pete and Pam. Congratulations to you both!

As investors, we know we have done a great job when the homeowners write us a thank-you letter. As you can see from the letter in Figure 5.17, this homeowner was very happy—another win-win situation.

FIGURE 5.2 Release Authorization

Gentlemen:

I give my permission for you to release any and all information
to _____*Pam*_____ regarding my property located at

' ████████*Stamford*_____

Ypsilanti MI 48198

in reference to any mortgage(s), liens or judgments. Please fax
a written payoff as of _____, 20___ to _____.
The fax number is (_____) _____.

✗SIGNED ██████████

CO-BORROWER _____

Borrower ████████
Address ████████ *St*
City/St/Zip ████████ *48103*
Bus. Phone _____ Res. Phone_____
✗S.S.# 3████████

Mortgagee *Citi Mortgage*
Address _____
Phone # *1-86*████████ Fax # ████████*431*
Loan # *2 00*████████ Contact_____

Now that you have seen just how easy it is to do short-sales,
let's go through the process step-by-step. Here is what you'll need to
get started:

> Phone log to track all your calls to the bank (see Figure 5.18).
> A signed "Authorization to Release Information" form.
> A signed sales contract with the price you are offering the bank.
> A hardship letter written by the homeowners.
> Proof of all hardships.
> Pictures of the disrepair.

FIGURE 5.3   Task/Phone Log

Current Owner(s) _____   Loan Number 200▒▒▒▒▒▒▒▒
Address of Property ▒▒▒▒▒▒▒▒▒ Superior Twp 48198

Date _____ Time _____ Company/Contact Name / Number _____
Task / Outcome _____

Date 11/9 ___ Time 8:40pm Company/Contact Name / Number Gurg transferred me to collections
Task / Outcome then to Loss Mitigation @ 866-▒▒▒▒▒▒▒▒ ext ▒▒▒▒ ≈ 7-4 oo.14

Date 11/29 ___ Time 4:04 AM Eastun Company/Contact Name / Number fax over cover / Listing agreemt /
Task / Outcome previous listing sheet, P.A., HUD
Dec 28th – Appraisal
happened
1 ▒▒▒▒ ▒▒▒▒▒▒▒ ▒▒▒ ▒▒▒

Date 1/4/07 Time 9:55am Company/Contact Name / Number talk to Nakeisha & she transferred me
Task / Outcome to Loss Mitigation @ Bld▒-▒▒▒▒▒▒▒ ext ▒▒▒▒▒ left message
w/ ▒▒▒▒▒▒▒▒▒, – ▒▒▒▒▒▒▒

Date 1/19/07 Time 12:54 Company/Contact Name / Number ▒▒▒▒▒▒▒▒ called back.
Task / Outcome 1-800-▒▒▒▒▒▒▒ ext. ▒▒▒▒

Date 1/19/07 Time _____ Company/Contact Name / Number talked to ▒▒▒▒▒ said offer has to go
Task / Outcome to PMI becus of such a shortage. + PMI has to go to Fannie Mae to get
approval.

Date 1/24/07 Time 2:12pm Company/Contact Name / Number talked to R▒▒ ▒▒▒▒ about property
Task / Outcome and she agreed to the bring a check for 2500 instead of promissory
note of 5000 for 60 mo. @ 0% interest for 83.33 per month.

Date 1/26/07 Time 9:59am Company/Contact Name / Number left message @ 800-▒▒▒▒▒▒▒▒ ext. 27
Task / Outcome to get final paperwork fax to do the deal

Date 1/26/07 Time 11:41am Company/Contact Name / Number ▒▒▒▒▒ called back & said we need
Task / Outcome close by February 19th ▒▒▒ MIP company said so. Do not use the 4 in
number when you call him. Also he should have paperwork for me today or monday
start title work going.

FIGURE 5.4 Formal Short-Sale Request

20 Øpages

Loan #: 200███████

Memorandum

To: ████@ Loss Mitigation *Michelle ████████*
            ███-███-████   *636-███-████*

From: Pamela Maddox
            Cell: 734-███████
            Fax: 734-███████

Re: Loan #: 200████████
            █████ Stamford Road
            Ypsilanti, MI 48198

Date: November 28, 2006

FORMAL REQUEST FOR SHORT SALE

Attached please find purchase agreement, HUD-1, listing agreement along with other documentation giving information regarding current market conditions in Michigan. These are the items that Mike in Loss Mitigations requested that I send to you. **This house has been on the market since 2004 consistently.** I have attached the MLS ticket. **The Purchaser is also able to buy the note on the above property and start & finish the foreclosure process.**

This homeowner has been trying to sell this house for quite sometime & has not had any offers. The reason for this is that the house is not in very good condition and the economy in Michigan is HORRIBLE. The house is in need of a roof and several other major items. Please read the attached documents and give me a call at the phone number listed above.

Authorization to Release Information

The "Authorization to Release Information" form is the only document that will allow you to speak directly with a lien holder about another's private account information. This must be delivered (usually via fax) to the lien holder before any information is released to you.

> ➤ Understand that this form does not authorize you to *do* anything on behalf of the homeowner, only to obtain information.

> ➤ Obtain a separate authorization to release for each lien holder. You can also use this authorization to obtain other information that may be helpful in negotiating the short-sale, including credit reports and medical records.

FIGURE 5.5   Sales Contract

ANN ARBOR AREA BOARD OF REALTORS®   **SALES CONTRACT • Page 1 of** _4_

Listing Office _Keller Williams_
Telephone _734_
Fax _734_
Listing Agent _Pam Thomas_
Telephone _734_
Fax _734_

Selling Office _X-odd Management_
Telephone ___
Fax ___
Selling Agent ___
Telephone _734_
Fax _734_

Email ___   Email ___

RE: THE PROPERTY KNOWN AS ___ _Stamford Rd_   _Superior Twp_   _48198_
(Street)   (City)   (Zip Code)

THIS CONTRACT is dated ___ _November 20, 2006_ ___ between

SELLER: _B___ ___s_
Address: ___ _Stamford Rd_   _Superior Twp 48198_   and
PURCHASER: _Gideon Group LLC +/or assigns_
Address: ___ _Main   Ann Arbor 48103_

Seller agrees to sell and convey, subject to easements and restrictive covenants of record, and subject to the lien of taxes not yet due and payable at time of closing, and Purchaser agrees to purchase the property situated in the ☐ City ☑ Twp of _Superior_ ___ County of _Washtenaw_ ___, Michigan, as identified above.

LEGAL DESCRIPTION: _L___ 55___ ___es #6_ ___ and will be completely described in the title insurance commitment.

SALE PRICE: _seventytwo thousand ————_ ^{xx}⁄₁₀₀ Dollars ($ _72,000.00_)

EARNEST MONEY: _ten ————_ ^{xx}⁄₁₀₀ Dollars ($ _10.00_)

Purchaser's earnest money will be deposited in the escrow account of ☐ Selling Broker, or ☐ Title Company, within two (2) banking days after Broker has received notice that an offer to purchase is accepted by all parties, until closing, at which time it will be credited to Purchaser. If this offer is not accepted, the earnest money will be returned in full to Purchaser.

FINANCING: ☐ Mortgage (see page 3) ☐ Land Contract (see Land Contract Addendum) ☑ Cash ☐ Other

FUNDS: Purchaser will pay the balance of the sale price, together with closing costs and escrow deposits, in collected funds at the time of closing. Purchaser is responsible for the performance of Purchaser's lender. Failure of the Purchaser's lender to have funds available for disbursement at the time of the scheduled closing may result in Purchaser's default.

OTHER CONDITIONS: _Seller agrees to waive proration of taxes_

Purchaser has a state of Michigan Real Estate License.

___
___
___

INCLUSIONS: This contract includes all fixtures, improvements, landscaping and appurtenances attached to the property as of this date, including but not limited to: all lighting and plumbing fixtures, ceiling fans, window treatments and hardware, wall-to-wall carpeting, attached shelving, purchased water softeners, automatic garage door equipment, storm

PURCHASERS' INITIALS _lulu_ ___   SELLERS' INITIALS ___

Use of this form is not authorized by the Ann Arbor Area Board of REALTORS® if standard form language is modified. Revised 10/05

___ 48097   Phone: (586) 751-0000   Fax: (731) 629-0665
___ Produced with zipForm™ by RE FormsNet, LLC 18025 Fifteen Mile Road, Clinton Township, Michigan 48035   www.zipform.com   peters

FIGURE 5.6 Property Listings: Recently Sold Comparable Properties (Comps)

Property Listing - Agent List With Photo Report

Select different report format

Off-Market Residential

Photo	Price Status MLS Prop. Type	Address City Area Number Map Coord	Beds Baths Style Sq.Ft.	Exterior Basement Garage Lot Sz./Ac.	Company Agent	Sold Price Closed Date Terms DOM	Multi Tour Map Relist
	$109,987 SOLD 542601823 RS	1300 WOODGLEN YPSILANTI 04151 AE - 15	3 1.1 1,331	60X110/0.15	Ehman & Greenstreet GMAC R.E. 734-482-3484 CLARK & JACK BROWN 734-216-7266	100,000 3/23/2006 CONV 41	☑ M N
	$117,350 SOLD 542516073 RS	2359 SUNNYGLEN AVENUE YPSILANTI 04151 A-E - 14	3 1.1 1,331	PART FIN, OTHER 1 CAR, ATT, ELECT, WORKSHP 60X105/0.14	Johnson & Associates Realty, I 734-761-2369 Gregory D. Johnson 734-657-0388	103,000 1/18/2006 CONV 1	☑ M N
	$114,900 SOLD 542603753 RS	1401 HARRY YPSILANTI 04151 AE - 15	3 1.1 · 1,470	FINISHED, OTHER 60 X 110/0	Keller Williams Ypsilanti 734-484-1800 DICK MATTIE 734-485-4232	105,000 7/31/2006 CONV 103	☑ M N
	$110,000 SOLD 25179108 RS	1568 STRATFORD CT SUPERIOR TWP 04151 AB - 14	3 1 OTHER 941	BRICK, ALUMINUM 2 CAR, ATT 69 X 116/0	FUTURE REAL ESTATE, INC 734-722-8500 TERRANCE HERMENAU 734-722-8500	110,400 5/8/2006 CASH 63	☑ M N
	$125,000 SOLD 542514873 RS	1647 FOLEY YPSILANTI 04151 AD - 14	3 1.1 1,347	62X100/0.15	The Charles Reinhart Company 734-480-4300 KYLE STONE 734-645-5788	125,000 5/12/2006 CONV 87	☑ M N
	$139,000 SOLD 25170923 RS	8668 KINGSTON CT SUPERIOR TWP 04151 -	2 2 SPLIT LEVEL 1,300	60 X 120/0	CENTURY 21 AMERICAL 734-676-2121 CHARLES MILLS 7346762121	139,000 11/27/2005 CONV 1	☑ M N
	$149,900 SOLD 542605416 RS	8671 PINE CT SUPERIOR 04101 AD - 12	3 1.1 1,300	BRICK, VINYL PART FIN, OTHER 1 CAR, ATT, ELECT 62 X 124/0	Keller Williams Ypsilanti 734-484-1800 DICK MATTIE 734-485-4232	149,900 8/11/2006 CONV 79	☑ A M N
	$159,900 SOLD 542513123 RS	8965 BRISTOL CT SUPERIOR 54062 000 - 0	3 1.1 1,300	OTHER FINISHED, OTHER 1 CAR, ATT, ELECT 68 X 136/0	Edward Surovoll Realtors 734-429-2200 KAREN BELLERS 734-741-5594	155,000 1/18/2006 CONV 77	☑ M N

Searching RS for
STATUS being either PEND or SOLD
AND AREA 04091, 54081, 54082, 54083, 54084, 54085, 54086, 54087, 54088, 54089, 04201, 04171, 04061, 54012, 04...
AND LISTING_TYPE being either A or Z
AND ARCHITECTURE being either D or F

FIGURE 5.7   News Article on Housing Prices

> IT'S ALWAYS A GREAT IDEA TO INCLUDE NEGATIVE INFORMATION ABOUT THE AREA. SHOWS THE BANK THAT IT MIGHT GET STUCK WITH THE PROPERTY.

Everything Michigan

THE ANN ARBOR NEWS

Listings rise, house prices fall   SHOWS
Average Washtenaw County sale drops over $10,000 since 2005

Wednesday, April 12, 2006

BY STEFANIE MURRAY

News Business Reporter

Does it seem like there are more "for sale" signs popping up in your neighborhood lately? You're not alone.

There are more homes for sale right now in Washtenaw County than some local Realtors say they can remember in more than 20 years. Meanwhile, sales have been flat.

More than 3,000 homes were listed for sale in the Ann Arbor-area during the first three months of 2006, up from 2,364 a year ago and 1,654 in 2001, the Ann Arbor Area Board of Realtors reported Tuesday. A total of 634 homes sold in the first quarter, up from 627 in the same period of 2005.

The average sale price of a home in the county decreased from $258,499 in 2005 to $247,683 this year. The median sale price dropped from $218,000 to $215,000.

Local real estate agents say the economy deserves the brunt of the blame for the increase in listings. Workers who've lost jobs recently or have felt their job security threatened amid Michigan's tough economic times want to downsize or cash out equity to pay bills.

"There is just so much inventory, it's just unbelievable," said Missy Caulk, a Realtor and broker with ReMax Platinum in Ann Arbor. "For buyers it means they have a lot of negotiating room and it means they have more choices," Caulk said. "For sellers, it basically means the competition is tough and that your house has to be in move-in condition."

And it has to be priced right. Across all price ranges, buyers are coming in with offers several thousand dollars below asking price – and they're not always willing to negotiate.

"It's definitely a buyers market right now, if you can even find a buyer," said Nelly Wisniewski, broker at Hometown One Inc. in Chelsea. "You really have to be very honest with people and let them know unless you want to sell your property at the bottom-line fair price, expect to have it sit there for six months to a year."

Total property sales during the first quarter - including vacant land, commercial properties and condos - dropped to 857 units sold from 877 in 2005.

Separately, sales of condos also fell slightly to 123 units sold from 134 a year ago. The median sale price of a condo fell to $164,900 from $180,300.

Michigan's housing market has certainly been much cooler than the rest of the nation.

While mortgage rates are moving up, home sales will stay near historically high levels in 2006, National Association of Realtors Chief Economist David Lereah said Tuesday.

Lereah expects the 30-year fixed-rate mortgage to rise to 6.9 percent by year end. The group forecasts existing home sales to drop 6 percent to 6.65 million units in 2006, down from a record 7.08 million in 2005.

Spring is typically a busy time for home sales, and despite the high number of listings, local agents say they're busy. Recent warm weather has helped.

FIGURE 5.8 Rehabbed House Exterior

The exact form that we use is shown in Figure 5.19. Feel free to make any changes necessary for your specific situation. Remember, use a different form for each lien holder.

Some lenders are now asking for notarized authorizations because too many investors have signed the homeowners' names without their permission. Imagine that!

Going to Contract

The next item you need from the homeowners is a signed sales contract (see Figures 5.20 and 5.21). There are several places you can get your hands on a contract. In our area, we can go to the local real estate board and buy directly. Check your area to see if this is

FIGURE 5.9   Homeowner's Hardship Letter

CitiMortgage
PO B████(██████)
Columbus, OH 43218-3040

December 7, 2006

Dear CitiMortgage:

I purchased the property located at ████ Stamford Road, Ypsilanti, MI 48198 in December 2002. Since this time, I have endured many hardships with this property (account number 2000████████). I purchased the property because at the time I was in a relationship with someone who promised to share in the responsibilities for the home. They were unable to purchase the home themselves. I was in the home until July of 2004. During this time my life was filled with broken financial commitments, and physical and verbal abuse. I was unable to get the person out of the home until November of 2004 because their name was placed on the deed.

I fell behind on the mortgage. The home was on the market previously, but I was unable to sell the property. I was able to get a renter for the home and catch back up on the mortgage. I tried to make a full commitment to make good on my loan with the home. I am unable to keep this up. The home is in need of major repairs (windows, roof, and doors), and I am not able to financially handle these burdens. During and since being in the home, my credit card debts are over $15,000. I can not keep up with the repairs for the home. The house is on the market for the second time. To date, no offers have been received. Please work with Pam, and remove this huge burdened from me. She will find someone who is willing to pay more than anyone else has offered for the property in its current condition.

Sincerely,

R████ ██████s

---

an option. You can also get contracts at local office supply stores as well as from attorneys.

TIP: A generic sales contract can be found at www.theieu.com.

FIGURE 5.10   Hardship Budget

Housing	Monthly Payment	Credit Cards	Monthly Payment
Rent/Mortgage	$820.54	Department store cards Kohl's	$550 / $21.00 per month
Heat	176.00	Visa	
Electric		Mastercard (Circid Cty)	$9,900 / $250 pymt
Water	$80.00 quarterly	Mastercard (mayic)	$1,300 / $21.00 pymt
House phone, 6bb Internet	$109.00	Visa	
Cell phone	$55.00	Miscellaneous	
Property Taxes (included of mortgage)		Discover	$5,000 / $10 pymt
Repairs & Improvements		Sears	$13,341.00
Garbage pickup		Home Depot	$1,500.00
Miscellaneous			
Food		**Car/Truck Payments**	
Groceries	$100.00	Payment 1	
Meals Out	Ø	Payment 2	
Mid-week shopping	Ø	Payment 3	
Paper/Cleaning/Grooming	Ø	Miscellaneous	
Miscellaneous	Ø		
Transportation		**Other Bills**	
Gas/Fares	$120.00	Attorney bill	$2,100
Auto Maintenance	Ø	College loan	$11,000
Parking	Ø	Personal loans	$3,500.00
Miscellaneous	Ø		
Insurance			
Car	$200. every six month		
House included in mortgage			
Life	Ø		
Miscellaneous	Ø		
Personal Expenses			
Clothing			
Medical Co-pays			
Dental			
Vision			
Gifts			
Donations			
Entertainment			
Child Care			
Vacations			
Haircuts/Laundry			
Pets			
Cable/Satellite			
Internet			
Tuition-college			
Alimony			

FIGURE 5.11   Market Decline Memorandum to the Appraiser

Memorandum

To: Chris @ ▓▓▓▓ Appraisals

From: Pamela Thomas
            Cell: 734▓▓▓
            Fax: 734▓▓▓

Re: ▓▓ Stamford Road
            Ypsilanti, MI 48198

Date: December 27, 2006

This neighborhood is going through a decline. The factors that is causing the area to decline is the

1. Availability of new housing nearby is great (the prices have dropped significantly on new construction)
   & because houses are not selling EVERYONE is trying to rent their homes until the market turns around.
2. Successive ownership of homes by lower income residents who are not maintaining their homes along with
   all the apartments located in the area
3. Many of the homes in this area have been converted to rental property.

Please take these things into consideration when doing your appraisal. This is a **short sale** not a refinance or a
first time purchase. This property has been on and off the market for over two years and has not sold yet – the
homeowners, as is everyone in Michigan, desperate.

I know that many appraisers are accustomed to give the highest value but please take into consideration the
factors I listed above as well as the comparables I have provided for you.

A note of caution for you: When investors use their own contracts, be sure to read them carefully for clauses that may not be favorable to you. Many times these contracts call for the buyer to:

➤ Pay all the closing costs (on both sides).

➤ Pay real estate taxes (prorated or not).

➤ Give up escrows.

In other words, these contracts are usually very one-sided. This is okay for you when selling, but not good when buying from others. We like to keep it simple and stick to the local common contract. We have never had a problem because of it.

When the bank entertains a short-sale, it must see that the seller is willing to sell at the lower price and walk away with no proceeds. The sale price on your sales contract is the amount you are offering the bank, not the balance on the mortgage.

FIGURE 5.12   Loan Payoff Acceptance Fax: The Bank Accepts Pete and Pam's Offer of $72,000

01/29/2007 13:31 FAX ████████   LOSS MITIGATION   ☑002/003

January 29, 2007

████████████

████████ST
███████, MI 48103-█

RE: ████7617

Dear Mortgagors,

CitiMortgage, Inc. has agreed to accept a short payoff on the above captioned loan with the following conditions:

1. The closing shall take place on or before February 15, 2007 or per diem interest in the amount of $75.00 will be charged. You must obtain approval from CitiMortgage, Inc. for any extension beyond February 23, 2007. Per diem interest will have to be absorbed by parties other then CitiMortgage, Inc..

2. CitiMortgage, Inc. net proceeds should not be less than $66,371.50. Contract price is $72,000.00.

3. Approved closing costs to be absorbed by CitiMortgage, Inc. including brokers commission are not to exceed $5,628.50. All other closing costs must be absorbed by parties other than CitiMortgage, Inc..

4. The current owners are to receive (0) zero proceeds from the sale of the above property. Any and all refunds or credits should be added to the net proceeds (from item #2 above) and remitted to CitiMortgage, Inc. at the time of closing.

5. Upon receipt of the NET PROCEEDS and a COPY OF THE FINAL SETTLEMENT STATEMENT, CitiMortgage, Inc. will give a full release and reconveyance of their loan as agreed and no deficiency judgment will be instituted.

6. All judgments and/or liens must be cleared and settled prior to closing. Proof of release must be presented at time of closing.

7. The current owner, ████████████ must bring certified funds in the amount of $2,500.00 to the closing. These funds must be certified and made payable to Republic Mortgage Insurance Company.

***ANY CHANGES TO THE ABOVE STATED TERMS MUST BE APPROVED BY CitiMortgage, Inc.

On the day of closing please fax a copy of the check along with a HUD 1 Settlement Statement to ████████

FIGURE 5.13   Additional Documents Request

01/29/2007 13:31 FAX ▓▓▓▓▓▓▓▓   LOSS MITIGATION   ▓ 003/003

Please forward THE N ET PROCEEDS CHECK, CERTIFIED CHECK MADE PAYABLE TO REPUBLIC MORTGAGE INSURANCE COMPANY with THE FINAL HUD1 SETTLEMENT STATEMENT to:

CitiMortgage, Inc.
1000 Technology Drive
O'Fallon, MO. 63368-2240
Attention: ▓▓▓▓▓▓▓▓

(VIA OVERNIGHT MAIL)

The loan will not be paid off without receipt of a Final Hud 1 settlement statement. Per diem interest will continue to accrue or proceeds check will be returned until all required documents have been received.

If you have any questions, please feel free to contact me at ▓▓▓▓▓▓ Ext▓▓ or ▓▓▓▓▓▓

Sincerely,

▓▓▓▓▓▓▓▓
Loss Mitigation Specia ist
CitiMortgage, Inc.
*Calls are randomly monitored and recorded to ensure quality service.

When you complete the sales contract, you are the buyer. It is best if you go to contract in a company name. If this is your first deal and you don't have a business entity yet, you could use your personal name. As soon as you have the funds, form a business entity. Business entities offer protection from lawsuits.

There are several ways to fill out a sales contract:

➤ *Personal name:* Use this option if you have not yet formed an entity.

➤ *Company name:* Make sure your company name sounds like a professional company, not a fly-by-night organization.

➤ *Real estate agent:* As an agent, you are considered a neutral third party. The bank knows you are trying to do what is best for the homeowners.

FIGURE 5.14 Purchaser's Statement

LIBERTY TITLE

PURCHASER'S STATEMENT

Borrower: Gideon Group, LLC
Seller: ▮▮▮▮▮▮▮▮
Settlement Agent: Liberty Title Agency
(734)665-6103
Place of Settlement: 111 N. Main Street
Ann Arbor, MI 48104
Settlement Date: February 13, 2007
Property Location: ▮▮▮ Stamford Road
Ypsilanti, MI 48198

DEBITS

Purchase Price		72,000.00
Commissions	Keller Williams Realty	610.50
	X - Odd - Management	
Loan Discount 2.9100 percent	Barbara Drake, Individual	2,700.00
Appraisal Fee	275.00	275.00
Settlement or Closing Fee	Liberty Title Agency	350.00
Title Insurance	Liberty Title Agency	250.80
Cashier Check Fee	Liberty Title Agency	25.00
Recording Fees	Washtenaw County Register of Deeds	61.00
Tax Certificate	Washtenaw Treasurer	1.00
Survey	Kem-Tec	95.00
Republic Mortgage Ins. Co.	Republic Mortgage Insurance Company	2,500.00
Gideon Group, LLC	Gideon Group, LLC	13,841.70
Gross Amount Due From Borrower	**TOTAL DEBITS**	92,710.00

CREDITS

Deposit or Earnest money		10.00
Principal Amount of New Loan(s)		92,700.00
Less Total Credits to Borrower	**TOTAL CREDITS**	92,710.00

BALANCE

APPROVED:

Gideon Group, LLC

▮▮▮▮▮▮▮ it's President

BROKER: Keller Williams Realty

Typically, we'll take the sales contract in our personal name initially, then change the name before the closing to one of our companies. Keep in mind that although you are out to create win-win situations, banks are seeking a one-way win and that's for them, so they will critique the offers as well as who the buyer is.

FIGURE 5.15   Seller's Statement

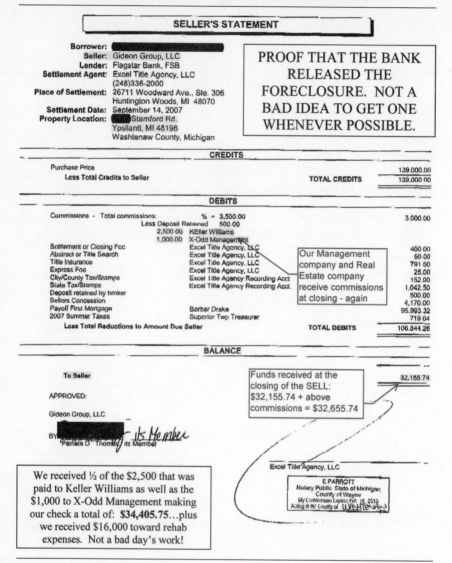

SELLER'S STATEMENT

Borrower:
Seller: Gideon Group, LLC
Lender: Flagstar Bank, FSB
Settlement Agent: Excel Title Agency, LLC
(248)336-2000
Place of Settlement: 26711 Woodward Ave., Ste. 306
Huntington Woods, MI 48070
Settlement Date: September 14, 2007
Property Location: Stamford Rd.
Ypsilanti, MI 48198
Washtenaw County, Michigan

PROOF THAT THE BANK RELEASED THE FORECLOSURE. NOT A BAD IDEA TO GET ONE WHENEVER POSSIBLE.

CREDITS

Purchase Price		139,000.00
Less Total Credits to Seller	TOTAL CREDITS	139,000.00

DEBITS

Commissions - Total commissions:	% = 3,500.00		3,000.00
	Less Deposit Retained 500.00		
	2,500.00 KEller Williams		
	1,000.00 X-Odd Management		
Settlement or Closing Fee	Excel Title Agency, LLC		400.00
Abstract or Title Search	Excel Title Agency, LLC		50.00
Title Insurance	Excel Title Agency, LLC		791.50
Express Fee	Excel Title Agency, LLC		25.00
City/County Tax/Stamps	Excel Title Agency Recording Acct		152.00
State Tax/Stamps	Excel Title Agency Recording Acct.		1,042.50
Deposit retained by broker			500.00
Sellers Concession			4,170.00
Payoff First Mortgage	Barbar Drake		95,993.32
2007 Summer Taxes	Superior Twp Treasurer		719.04
Less Total Reductions to Amount Due Seller		TOTAL DEBITS	106,844.26

Our Management company and Real Estate company receive commissions at closing - again

BALANCE

To Seller	
APPROVED:	32,155.74
Gideon Group, LLC	
BY its Member	
Pamela D Thomas / its Member	

Funds received at the closing of the SELL: $32,155.74 + above commissions = $32,655.74

Excel Title Agency, LLC

E PARROTT
Notary Public State of Michigan
County of Wayne
My Commission Expires Feb 15, 2013
Acting in the County of WASHTENAW

We received ½ of the $2,500 that was paid to Keller Williams as well as the $1,000 to X-Odd Management making our check a total of: **$34,405.75**...plus we received $16,000 toward rehab expenses. Not a bad day's work!

A per diem rate is the penalty for closing past the specified date. This way if you need an extra period of time, you'll have it. If the per diem rate is $65 per day and you run 10 days late, you would owe an additional $650. Call the bank right before the closing and re-negotiate the short-sale per diem charge.

FIGURE 5.16   Certificate of Discharge

CERTIFICATE OF DISCHARGE

CITIMORTGAGE, INC. #:2000████████RS" Lender ████████ Washtenaw, Michigan
KNOW ALL MEN BY THESE PRESENTS that CITIMORTGAGE, INC. whose address is 5280 CORPORATE DRIVE, MC 22-528-1020, FREDERICK, MD 21703 current holder of a certain Mortgage, whose parties, dates and recording information are below, does hereby acknowledge that it has received full payment and satisfaction of the same, and in consideration thereof, does hereby cancel and discharge said Mortgage.

Original Grantor: █████████████████
Original Grantee: TH████████████, GROUP
Dated: 12/23/2002
Date Recorded: 01/03/2003 In Book/Reel/Liber: ███████████████████████████086
In the County of Washtenaw State of Michigan

Property Address: ████ STAMFORD RD, YPSILANTI, MI 48198-3243

IN WITNESS WHEREOF, CITIMORTGAGE, INC., by the officer duly authorized, has duly executed as a free act and deed the foregoing instrument;

CITIMORTGAGE, INC.
On February 20th, 2007

By: _____
MICHELLE R FORD, Vice-President

CITIMORTGAGE, INC.
CORPORATE
SEAL
NEW YORK

STATE OF Maryland
COUNTY OF Frederick

On February 20th, 2007, before me, SANDRA FOGLE, a Notary Public in and for Frederick in the State of Maryland, personally appeared MICHELLE R FORD, Vice-President, personally known to me (or proved to me on the basis of satisfactory evidence) to be the person(s) whose name(s) is/are subscribed to the within instrument and acknowledged to me that he/she/they executed the same in his/her/their authorized capacity, and that by his/her/their signature on the instrument the person(s), or the entity upon behalf of which the person(s) acted, executed the instrument.

WITNESS my hand and official seal,

_____
SANDRA FOGLE
Notary Expires: 05/09/2007

SANDRA FOGLE
NOTARY PUBLIC
FREDERICK CO., MD

Prepared By: SHERRY SHEFFLER, VERDUGO TRUSTEE SERVICE CORPORATION PO BOX 9443, GAITHERSBURG, MD 20898-9443 1-800-283-7918
When Recorded Return To: ████████████████████████████████████243

SUBMITTED
FOR
SUBMITTED
FOR RECORDING

FEB 2 6 2007

Washtenaw County, MI
Clerk Register's Office

*LMA*LMACITM*02/19/2007 03:50:00 PM* CITM01CITM00000000000000002824156* MIWASHT* 2000587617 MISTATE_MORT_REL *MD1*MO1CITM*

FIGURE 5.17   Happy Customer Letter: Thank-You Letter from the Homeowner to Pam

February 17, 2007

Pam Thomas, Agent
K̶̶̶̶̶̶̶̶

Dear Pam:

I want to express my sincere appreciation for all of your hard work. When I came to you with my situation you were caring, understanding and very helpful. Because of my circumstance you jumped right in and starting working on the sale of my house.

You worked relentlessly to settle this matter in an extremely short period of time. I could always call you with questions, concerns or problems I was experiencing due to the sale of this house. Pam, you walked me through the process. Informing me of any changes, and letting me know what you needed from me. You took on all the headaches that I would have had, and for that I am truly grateful. Your knowledge of your profession is obvious, and can be seen in your every day work dealings.

I thank you again for all that you have done. My life was made alot easier due to meeting you. I will recommend you to anyone that I encounter that is in need of your service.

Sincerely,

R̶̶̶̶̶̶̶̶
Very Happy Client

TIP: Always ask the bank what its per diem rate is.

Hardship Letter

The hardship letter is a must. It must be written by the homeowners, state the reasons for the distress, and explain why the bank should accept less as payment in full. Anything stated in this letter that can be backed up with proof should be.

FIGURE 5.18   Sample Acquisition Phone Log (Downloadable*)

CURRENT OWNER _____

LOAN NUMBER _____

ADDRESS OF PROPERTY _____

DATE _____ TIME ____ COMPANY/CONTACT _____

OUTCOME _____

DATE _____ TIME ____ COMPANY/CONTACT _____

OUTCOME _____

DATE _____ TIME ____ COMPANY/CONTACT _____

OUTCOME _____

DATE _____ TIME ____ COMPANY/CONTACT _____

OUTCOME _____

DATE _____ TIME ____ COMPANY/CONTACT _____

OUTCOME _____

*Copyright © 2008 by Dwan Bent-Twyford and Sharon Restrepo. To download and customize this form for your personal use, please visit www.theieu.com/shortsaleform.

For example:

➤ If the homeowner has medical conditions and/or bills, enclose doctors' letters and medical bills, using a separate "Authorization to Release Information" form to obtain this information.

➤ If there has been a divorce affecting income, obtain the decree.

➤ If the sellers' credit is shot, then obtain a copy of their credit report.

➤ If they have filed bankruptcy, include proof.

You get the idea. Figures 5.9 and 5.22 are examples of hardship letters. You may have to help the homeowners with the letter by pointing out the distress. Many times when people have lived in a

FIGURE 5.19   Sample Release Authorization Form (Downloadable*)

To Whom It May Concern:

I give my permission for you to release any and all information to [YOU—THE INVESTOR] regarding my property located at [1279 Smith Street, Dayton, Ohio 45388] in reference to any mortgage(s), liens or judgments, or bankruptcy process.

SIGNED _____ CO-BORROWER _____

Borrower _____

Address _____ City/St/Zip _____

Bus. Phone _____ Res. Phone _____

S.S. # _____

Mortgagee _____

Phone # _____ Fax # _____

Loan # _____ Contact _____

*Copyright © 2008 by Dwan Bent-Twyford and Sharon Restrepo. To download and customize this form for your personal use, please visit www.theieu.com/shortsaleform.

property for a long time, they no longer see the disrepair. Don't be worried about hurting their feelings; this letter is a key factor to your being able to help them.

We typically ask for a five- or six-page letter. Homeowners writing a hardship letter tend to write only a few sentences. When you ask for five or six pages, you might get two or three pages. Make certain that the letters are very detailed.

As you can see, these letters are pretty sad. The better the letter explains the homeowners' hardship, the better your chances of getting your short-sale accepted. The bank needs to see that the homeowner *cannot* afford to keep the property. If the bankers think for one minute that the homeowner just doesn't want it anymore, they will say no.

Banks base everything on the numbers. We try to put some emotion into the deal. When the homeowners write a sad letter and back it up with proof, it typically gets the loss mitigation rep emotionally involved in the outcome. When the reps feel sympathy for the homeowners, they are more likely to help you with the short-sale.

FIGURE 5.20   Sample Contract Information (Downloadable*)

Seller:	Mr. and Mrs. Distressed Homeowners
Buyer:	You, the investor. You can put the contract in your personal name and actually close in a different name. We often do this because we don't want the bank to think that we are savvy investors initially. We use our personal name on the contract and then close in the corporate name. The lenders usually have no problem with this.

Property

Address:	Address of the property you are planning to purchase.
Price:	This number is the amount you are offering the bank. We offer approximately 40 percent of the retail value **or less as a starting point**.
Deposit:	**You are to give a $10 deposit.** If the homeowners are uncomfortable with this amount, explain to them that the banks do not allow the homeowners to profit from the bank's loss; therefore, you cannot give a larger deposit.
Terms:	Closing based on lender's acceptance of your offer. All cash, as-is condition.

Closing

Date:	**On or before** 30 days from the bank's acceptance.

*Copyright © 2008 by Dwan Bent-Twyford and Sharon Restrepo. To download and customize this form for your personal use, please visit www.theieu.com/shortsaleform.

In all hardship letters, the homeowners should mention filing bankruptcy if they are planning to. The banks know that a homeowner with a good attorney can file bankruptcy and buy up to two years or more of *free living* during which the bank cannot take the house in foreclosure.

Earlier (in Chapter 2) we told you that many banks have to keep a cash reserve of unlendable money for each property they own. If a bank knows a piece of property will be tied up in bankruptcy for two years and that the homeowners are in distress, it is likely to accept the short-sale instead of waiting out the bankruptcy process so it can free up its money.

FIGURE 5.21   Sample Contract for Sale and Purchase (Downloadable*)

Buyer   _____

(address) _____

and

Seller   _____

(address) _____

do hereby agree that the Seller shall sell and the Buyer shall buy the following property UPON THE TERMS AND CONDITIONS HEREINAFTER SET FORTH, which shall include the STANDARDS FOR REAL ESTATE TRANSACTIONS set forth within this contract.

[IN THIS SECTION, CHECK ALL ITEMS THAT WILL REMAIN WITH THE PROPERTY.]

Personal Property Included: All fixed equipment, all window screens, treatments and hardware, all wall-to-wall floor coverings, attached wall coverings, and attached lighting fixtures as now installed on said property. Also included are the indicated major appliances: range_____, refrigerator_____, dishwasher_____, disposal_____, microwave oven_____, trash compactor_____, washer_____, dryer_____.

Additional Personal Property Included: _____

1. **LEGAL DESCRIPTION** of real estate located in _____
    County, State of _____:

    Legal description:

    [WHEN BUYING, GIVE $10. WHEN SELLING TO A REHABBER OR END USER, TAKE AT LEAST $2,500.]

2. PURCHASE PRICE $ _____
(a) Deposit $ _____
    Deposit to be held in trust by: _____
    YOUR TITLE COMPANY _____

FIGURE 5.21   *(Continued)*

[NO ADDITIONAL DEPOSIT, CONTRACT IS AS-IS FULL DEPOSIT IS DUE NOW.]

(b) Additional deposit due within _____ days after date of acceptance. Time is of the essence as to additional deposit. $ _____

[IN THIS SECTION, MARK EVERYTHING "N/A". WE ARE NOT ACCEPTING CONTRACTS BASED ON FINANCING.]

(c) Amount of new note and mortgage to be executed by the Buyer to any Lender other than the Seller. New note to be adjustable rate _____ or fixed rate _____.

$_____ FHA _____ VA _____ (if applicable)

(d) Approximate additional payment due at closing in U.S. currency or LOCAL cashier's check (does not include buyer's closing costs and/or prepaid items).

$ _____

3. PRORATIONS: Taxes, insurance, interest, rents, and other expenses and revenue of said property shall be prorated as of the date of closing.

4. RESTRICTIONS, EASEMENTS, LIMITATIONS: Buyer shall take title subject to: (a) Zoning, restrictions, prohibitions and requirements imposed by governmental authority, (b) Restrictions and matters appearing on the plat or common to the subdivision, (c) Public utility easements of record, provided said easements are located on the side or rear lines of the property, (d) Taxes for year of closing, assumed mortgages, and purchase money mortgages, if any, (e) Other _____.

    Seller warrants that there shall be no violations of building or zoning codes at the time of closing.

5. DEFAULT BY BUYER: If the Buyer fails to perform any of the covenants of this contract, all money paid pursuant to this contract by Buyer as previously mentioned shall be retained by or for the account of the Seller as consideration for the execution of this contract and as agreed liquidated damages and in full settlement of any claims for damages.

(Continued)

FIGURE 5.21   (Continued)

6. DEFAULT BY SELLER: If the Seller fails to perform any of the covenants of this contract, the aforesaid money paid by the Buyer, at the option of the Buyer, shall be returned to the Buyer on demand; or the Buyer shall have only the right of specific performance.

[IN THE NEXT FEW SECTIONS, LEAVE THE INSPECTION CLAUSES IN WHEN BUYING AND OUT WHEN SELLING.]

["Z" THIS SECTION OUT. PLACE THE INITIALS "N/A" OVER THE "Z." PROPERTY IS BEING SOLD IN AS-IS CONDITION.]

7. TERMITE INSPECTION: At least 15 days before closing, Buyer, at Buyer's expense, shall have the right to obtain a written report from a licensed exterminator stating that there is no evidence of live termite or other woodboring insect infestation on said property nor substantial damage from prior infestation on said property. If there is such evidence, Seller shall pay up to two (2%) percent of the purchase price for the treatment required to remedy such infestation, including repairing and replacing portions of said improvements which have been damaged; but if the costs for such treatment or repairs exceed three (3%) percent of the purchase price, Buyer may elect to pay such excess. If Buyer elects not to pay, Seller may pay the excess or cancel the contract.

["Z"THIS SECTION OUT ("N/A") PROPERTY IS BEING SOLD IN AS-IS CONDITION.]

8. ROOF INSPECTION: At least 15 days before closing, Buyer, at Buyer's expense, shall have the right to obtain a written report from a licensed roofer stating that the roof is in a watertight condition. In the event repairs are required either to correct leaks or to repair damage to fascia or soffit, Seller shall pay up to two percent (2%) of the purchase price for said repairs, which shall be performed by a licensed roofing contractor; but if the costs for such repairs exceeds three percent (3%) of the purchase price, Buyer may elect to pay such excess. If Buyer elects not to pay, Seller may pay the excess or cancel the contract.

["Z" THIS SECTION OUT ("N/A") PROPERTY IS BEING SOLD IN AS-IS CONDITION.]

FIGURE 5.21 *(Continued)*

9. OTHER INSPECTIONS: At least 15 days before closing, Buyer or his agent may inspect all appliances, air-conditioning and heating systems, electrical systems, plumbing, machinery, sprinklers, and pool system included in the sale. Seller shall pay for the repairs necessary to place such items in working order at the time of closing. Within 48 hours before closing, Buyer shall be entitled, upon reasonable notice to Seller, to inspect the premises to determine that said items are in working order. All items of personal property included in the sale shall be transferred by Bill of Sale with warranty of title.

10. LEASES: Seller, not less than 15 days before closing, shall furnish to Buyer copies of all written leases and estoppel letters from each tenant specifying the nature and duration of the tenant's occupancy, rental rates and advanced rent and security deposits paid by tenant. If Seller is unable to obtain such letters from tenants, Seller shall furnish the same information to Buyer within said time period in the form of a Seller's affidavit, and Buyer may contact tenants thereafter to confirm such information. At closing, Seller shall deliver and assign all original leases to Buyer.

11. MECHANICS' LIENS: Seller shall furnish to Buyer an affidavit that there have been no improvements to the subject property for 90 days immediately preceding the date of closing, and no financing statements, claims of lien, or potential lienors known to Seller. If the property has been improved within that time, Seller shall deliver releases or waivers of all mechanics' liens as executed by general contractors, subcontractors, suppliers, and materialmen and reciting that all bills for work to the subject property which could serve as basis for mechanics' liens have been paid or will be paid at closing.

[CLOSING IS ALWAYS TO BE AT YOUR TITLE COMPANY.]

12. PLACE OF CLOSING: Closing shall be held at the office of the Seller's attorney or as otherwise agreed upon.

13. TIME IS OF THE ESSENCE: Time is of the essence of this Sale and Purchase Agreement.

14 DOCUMENTS FOR CLOSING: Seller's attorney shall prepare deed, note, mortgage, Seller's affidavit, any corrective instruments required for perfecting the title, and closing statement, and submit copies of same to Buyer's attorney,

(Continued)

FIGURE 5.21   *(Continued)*

and copy of closing statement to the broker, at least two days prior to scheduled closing date.

15. EXPENSES: State documentary stamps required on the instrument of conveyance and the cost of recording any corrective instruments shall be paid by Seller. Documentary stamps to be affixed to the note secured by the purchase money mortgage shall be paid by Buyer.

16. INSURANCE: If insurance is to be prorated, the Seller shall on or before the closing date furnish to Buyer all insurance policies or copies thereof.

17. RISK OF LOSS: If the improvements are damaged by fire or casualty before delivery of the deed and can be restored to substantiality the same condition as now within a period of 60 days thereafter, Seller shall so restore the improvements and the closing date and date of delivery of possession herein provided shall be extended accordingly. If Seller fails to do so, the Buyer shall have the option of (1) taking the property as-is, together with insurance proceeds, if any, or (2) canceling the contract, and all deposits shall be forthwith returned to the Buyer and all parties shall be released of any and all obligations and liability.

18. MAINTENANCE: Between the date of the contract and the date of closing, the property, including lawn, shrubbery, and pool, if any, shall be maintained by Seller in the condition as it existed as of the date of the contract, ordinary wear and tear excepted.

[ALWAYS WRITE THE WORDS "ON OR BEFORE" IF THEY ARE NOT ALREADY WRITTEN INTO THE CONTRACT. NEVER ALLOW "ON OR ABOUT" TO BE THE CLOSING DATE. "ON OR ABOUT" COULD BE LATER AND YOU MAY NOT HAVE TIME DUE TO THE SHERIFF'S SALE.]

19. CLOSING DATE: This contract shall be closed and the deed and possession shall be delivered on or before the _____ day of _____ , unless extended by other provisions of this contract.

20. TYPEWRITTEN OR HANDWRITTEN PROVISIONS: Typewritten or handwritten provisions inserted in this form shall control all printed provisions in conflict therewith.

FIGURE 5.21   (Continued)

21. OTHER AGREEMENTS: No agreements or representations, unless incorporated in this contract, shall be binding upon any of the parties.

[BELOW ARE SOME OF THE CLAUSES I USE.]

22 SPECIAL CLAUSES:

1.   One of the buyers/sellers is a [your state] licensed real estate agent.

2.   Buyer (rehabber) agrees to purchase subject property in "as-is, where-is" condition.

3.   Buyer (rehabber) agrees and understands that Seller (you, the wholesaler) has never lived in subject property and guarantees or warrants nothing.

4.   All parties agree that [your closing agent] will act as closing agent.

5.   Seller (homeowner) acknowledges that Buyer (wholesaler) is an investor and intends to resell subject property for a profit as soon as possible.

6.   Transaction is contingent upon the ability of Seller (you, the wholesaler) to transfer title on or before the stated closing date, as Seller (you, the wholesaler) is not owner of record (the homeowner is) and must close with owner of record (homeowner) first.

COMMISSION TO BROKER: The Seller hereby recognizes _____ as the Broker in this transaction, and agrees to pay as commission _____% of the gross sale price, or the sum of _____ dollars ($_____), or one-half of the deposit in case same is forfeited by the Buyer through failure to perform, as compensation for services rendered, provided same does not exceed the full amount of the commission.

SIGNATURES:

_____

_____

_____

My partner and I purchased a property for $42,000. We whole-saled it for $75,000. After giving the homeowners some money, I made $13,000 on the deal and my partner made $10,000. It was so fast and easy. Thanks, Dwan & Sharon!

Doug L., Texas

FIGURE 5.22   Sample Homeowner Hardship Letter (Downloadable*)

[Name and address of bank]

Loan #_____

Dear [bank contact's name]:

I am writing this letter to share some of the hardships I have endured over the past year. As you know, my property located at [address] is currently facing foreclosure. I have tried to sell the property for months and have gotten only one serious offer because of the poor condition of the property. Based on the offer I have, I urge you to please accept the [amount] being submitted by [name of investor].

Please accept this offer as payment in full. My attorney has advised me to file bankruptcy, but I prefer to avoid further destruction of my credit. I just want to move on and start over.

I am enclosing my bank statements from the past three months, late notices on my car, and anything else I can find that shows the financial trouble I'm facing. I have also enclosed my last year's tax returns.

I am in the [name of] industry and am currently looking for another field in which to work. So far, I haven't had much success.

If there is any other information you need, please feel free to call me.

Sincerely,

[Name of homeowner]

Pictures

This is your opportunity to make your case for a short-sale! Take pictures of any disrepair or damage you can find.

Take pictures on the first visit so you don't have to return.

TIP: It is helpful to take pictures with a digital camera, because they can be e-mailed directly to the loss mitigation rep.

Another benefit to digital pictures is that you can input them into your computer and insert words on them to describe the damage in the picture. Regular pictures will work, but be sure to develop doubles so that if the bank misplaces them, you have backup.

TIP: If you send pictures through the mail, get a tracking number so you can find out who signed for them and be certain they got to the right person.

If the property has no disrepair, don't send any pictures. Whatever does not help your case hurts it. Pictures of a beautiful property will not help your case.

Regardless of the condition of the property, you can still do the short-sale. Banks accept short-sales on pretty houses all day long. A pretty house is still a liability to the bank. The reasons we mentioned in the beginning of this book as to why banks accept short-sales still stand regardless of the condition of the property.

The photograph in Figure 5.23 speaks a thousand words. Do you think this homeowner has some anger management issues?

The room shown in Figure 5.24 looks like a fun room to start with.

After looking at these pictures, any banker would give your offer serious consideration. Remember, banks are in the business of lending money, not rehabbing houses.

Investor Cover Letter

Start your package with a cover letter justifying your offer, and include all the items we have listed in your package.

FIGURE 5.23   Exterior of House in Bad Shape

Don't forget to ask the banks to waive the **deficiency judgment** in your cover letters. Allow the sellers to give you permission after seeking advice from their tax expert.

Deficiency judgment   When a bank takes a short-sale, it has the right to pursue the homeowners for any shortage of the mortgage balance. As an example, a homeowner has a property worth $200,000 with a $200,000 mortgage balance. The bank agrees to accept $100,000 as full payment. But the bank can then pursue the homeowners for the $100,000 loss by way of deficiency judgment. This means the homeowners now have a judgment of $100,000 against them that will have to be paid in order for them to move on. The homeowners can try to negotiate the judgment down to a lower amount and pay it off or file bankruptcy with an attorney to wipe it out completely.

FIGURE 5.24   Room in Bad Shape

Figure 5.25 shows a sample cover letter we have used with great success. As you can see, this letter is strong and justifies our low offer. The bold is to remind you to include these sentences in your letters should you write your own letters.

Since our goal is to create a win-win situation, we always try to get the homeowners a clean slate. Most of the time, the banks will agree to this. Our goal is to help the homeowners start their lives over. Leaving them with a huge deficiency judgment or a tax liability will not make their situation better.

Comps That Justify Your Offer

You definitely want to include comparable sales for the subject property in the area. Comps, as they're called, are properties that have

FIGURE 5.25   Sample Cover Letter (Downloadable*)

FORMAL REQUEST FOR SHORT SALE

[Date]

Loan Number_____

Dear [bank contact's name]:

As you know, the property of [distressed homeowners' names], located at [address and loan number], is facing foreclosure. I am trying to help them out of this dilemma. At this time, it seems as though the only solution is for them to sell their property.

Upon my inspection, I find that the property needs a lot of work to bring it up to current market standards. I called a real estate agent in this area and requested current market values and have based my offer on the market values as well as the necessary repairs. **Based on the area comps, you can see [distressed homeowners' names] owe you far more than their property is worth.**

My offer is [amount] cash as payment in full inclusive of all fees, taxes, etc. I am prepared to close in [amount of time]. **We also ask that you waive any deficiency judgment against [distresed homeowners' names].**

Please review the attached documents and respond at your earliest convenience. We urge you to accept our proposal and move for a quick closing on this property.

Thank you for your cooperation. I look forward to working with you to help [distressed homeowners' names].

Sincerely,

[Your name]

sold within the past six months that compare most closely to the property you are negotiating. You can obtain comps yourself from an online service, from a real estate agent or associate, or from a title company.

On one of my first wholesale deals, I secured a property by purchasing a $70,000 delinquent mortgage note for $5,000 and taking a deed in lieu of foreclosure (a technique learned in your course). I then negotiated over $310,000 in municipal liens down to $7,500 (also a technique learned in your course), and finally, I sold the property wholesale (certainly one of the best things learned in your course!) to a local rehabber. After leaving a substantial profit for him, I made over $40,000. I did all this on a house that had been abandoned for years, used as a crack house, and passed over by literally hundreds of other investors. Thank you, Sharon & Dwan!

Forever your student,
Stephen Denny, Florida

I found a property that I paid $65,000 for. I wholesaled it for $79,000. After some closing costs and giving the homeowners some money to start over with, I netted $6,612 on my first deal. The whole process took only 43 days. I saved the homeowners and the bank from a foreclosure filing. The homeowners felt blessed to be able to walk away and not have a foreclosure on their record. Everybody won. It was great!

Marty Joe, Ohio

TIP: Remember, these comps must help justify the sale price you are asking the bank to accept.

It is best to send the comps on the forms an actual real estate agent would use.

Again, the comps will be based on sales in your market, whether a $100,000 neighborhood or an $800,000 neighborhood.

If you were offering $40,000 on a property worth $100,000 in mint condition, the following comps would certainly justify your offer:

Area Comps: 382 N.W. 18th Street, City of Subject Property

Address	Date Sold	Amount
926 N.W. 18th St.	Recent	$39,000 WD
267 N.W. 16th St.	Recent	$35,000 CT
687 N.W. 27th St.	Recent	$29,000 CT
567 N.W. 14th St.	Recent	$9,000 SW
126 N.W. 25th St.	Recent	$35,000 QC
851 N.W. 15th St.	Recent	$37,000 WD

TIP: Try to use comps that are no more than six months old.

By designating QC (quitclaim deed), SW (special warranty deed), and CT (certificate of title), you show the bank that the neighborhood is not stable. These types of deeds are usually related to a distressed property. Special warranty and quitclaim deeds are typically deeds from a sheriff's sale. Remember that a true comp is a property of similar condition and situation. Even though a home may be in great condition, a comp would be one in a similar situation. That's why unique transfer types, as mentioned earlier, are valid comps.

If you cannot find any justifying comps, then leave them out.

TIP: Remember, you are building a case. If comps don't help you, they hurt you. Do not include anything in your package unless it helps your case.

For distressed properties, use comps that are similar homes in similar condition like handyman specials and foreclosures. Homes that have manicured lawns are not similar and will not help you obtain your goal.

If the comps you are using were provided by a real estate agent, then include that agent's name and number as a reference for the bank to speak to about the market value.

Typically, even though you send the bank comps and a list of needed repairs, the bank will order its own appraisal on the property. Because you are the contact person, the appraiser will call you to arrange the time to get in and appraise the home.

We'll talk more about this later.

Net Sheet

The net sheet is a form that shows the bank what it will net from your offer. The net sheet is a quick and simple form to use during the negotiating process. At closing, the closing agent will use a more comprehensive form known as a closing or settlement statement, or HUD-1. It's fine to use any of the above during negotiations.

> ➤ For example, if we offered you $150,000 for your home and you agreed, would you leave the closing with the entire $150,000? No, because you would have to pay some closing costs.

Because of the homeowners' distress, the bank steps into the homeowners' shoes at the closing. In other words, the bank pays any closing costs the homeowners are required to pay.

FIGURE 5.26   Sample Net Sheet (Downloadable*)

Account #_____

Sale Price	$150,000
Commission	0
Documentary Stamps	1,050
Abstract Title	275
Title to Close	175
Real Estate Taxes	3,400
Miscellaneous Costs	1,500
Total Closing Costs	**$6,400**
Approximate Net to Bank	**$143,600**

*Copyright © 2008 by Dwan Bent-Twyford and Sharon Restrepo. To download and customize this form for your personal use, please visit www.theieu.com/shortsaleform.

➤ The bank will be covering the closing costs, real estate taxes, real estate commissions, and so forth and will actually net a figure other than the offer price.

In the sample net sheet shown in Figure 5.26, the bank will base its decision on $143,600 instead of $150,000. If $143,600 is acceptable, you have a deal.

TIP: When first starting out, you can get these closing cost figures from a title company, a closing agent, an attorney, or online.

As you close more deals you will learn these closing cost figures. The banks are not looking for exact amounts, just close estimates. They will usually look at your net sheet and approve a figure that is an actual net to them regardless of the closing costs.

Any additional costs would come from your side, which will add to the amount you have agreed to pay.

Estimated List and Cost of Repairs

Next, we'll discuss your repairs list. Even with a nice property there are still repairs to be done. That's because most properties usually need a new coat of interior and exterior paint, new appliances, fixture replacements, and other items.

TIP: Simply updating the bathrooms and kitchen and replacing carpets can add up to $20,000 or more to your repair costs.

When you are starting out you may not know what repairs cost. A great way to learn these figures is to visit your local home repair store and ask the employees what it costs to update kitchens, replace carpets, or install a new garage door. These folks are usually very helpful. Many of these stores offer classes that teach you how to do the repairs as well as what it costs should you hire it out.

Every investor should know the costs of basic repairs. If you don't know these numbers, how will you know if you are getting ripped off when you have work done? Take time to learn this part of our business.

If you use particular contractors and other workers, you can use their estimates on their professional stationery. Contractors' estimating forms are available at your local office supply store.

Be sure to include a detailed list of everything both interior and exterior, from roof to basement. You want to build a good case.

A sample repairs list is shown in Figure 5.27.

FIGURE 5.27   Sample Repairs List (Downloadable*)

CUSTOMIZE FOR YOURSELF!

Roof: The existing roof is an extremely old cement tile roof, which must be replaced with a new asphalt shingle roof. Also, the flat roof over the addition must be redone.

Approx.:_____$5,000.00_

Wood Rot/Fascia/Soffits: There is evidence of live termite infestation and over 40 percent of the fascia and soffits must be replaced when the existing roof is torn off.

Approx.:_____$ 650.00 for the termite tent._

Approx.:_____$1,900.00 for wood replacement & labor._

Flooring: Existing carpet is torn and/or missing in various places; padding does not meet FHA standards. Must recarpet or tile.

Approx.:_____$1,750.00_

Doors: Closet doors are missing and should be replaced.

Approx.:_____$ 700.00_

Exterior: Carport area/laundry room—doors are missing and must be replaced; cost included in other quotes.

Approx.:_____$2,200.00_

Paint: Interior paint (including ceiling patches, etc.) and exterior pressure cleaning and painting are required.

Approx.:_____$2,700.00_

Windows: All windows are original jalousie panes, which are outdated and extremely energy inefficient.

Approx.:_____$3,200.00_

Bath(s):   Plumbing fixtures leak and must be replaced.

Approx.:_____$ 475.00_

***Possible Code Violation** exists due to an addition on the rear of the property that does not meet current code requirements.

Approx. cost to bring to code or remove:_$6,500.00_

Approximate Total: $25,075.

*Please note that these quotes do not include any structural problems.

FIGURE 5.28   Sample Property Information Sheet (Downloadable*)

Date _____

Owner Name _____

Property Address _____

_____

Property Type: Single-Family_____; Duplex _____;Triplex _____;
Multi-Unit _____;Two-Story_____; Single-Level_____; Beds_____;
Baths_____

Roads: Paved_____; Unpaved_____

Special Features:

       Fireplace—How many_____;Where _____

       Attached Garage—Single car, Double car, Other

       Detached Garage—Single car, Double car, Other

       Carport—Single car, Double car, Other

       Waterfront—Lake, Canal, Ocean, River

       Pool—In ground, Above ground, Size _____

       Jacuzzi—Attached to pool, Separate

       Covered Patio _____

       Screened Porch _____

       Ceiling Fans—How many? _____;Where _____

       Irrigation System _____

       Central Heat/Air _____

       Intercom System _____

       Fenced Yard _____

       Central Vacuum System _____

       Other _____

(Continued)

FIGURE 5.28   *(Continued)*

Year Built _____; Square Footage: _____; Lot Size _____;

Taxes _____; Taxes Current? Yes/No

Exterior Condition: Poor _____; Good _____; Great _____

Roof: Good _____; Needs work _____; Needs to be replaced _____

Exterior Paint: Good _____; New paint required _____

Termite Damage: Where and how much _____

Condition of Yard: _____

Windows: _____

Interior Condition: Poor _____; Good _____; Great _____

Kitchen: Outdated _____; Not working condition _____; Replace

appliances _____; Replace cabinets _____; Replace flooring _____;

Other _____

Baths: Outdated _____; Not working condition _____; Replace tub/

shower _____; Replace cabinets _____; Replace flooring _____;

Other _____

Flooring: Type _____; Condition _____; Rooms to be

replaced _____;

Paint: Describe what needs to be done to bring to current standards:

_____

Walls and Ceilings: Describe condition and what to do:

_____

Number of listings in area: _____

Average price range: _____

Number of days on market: _____

General appearance of neighborhood: _____

We use the form shown in Figure 5.28 to track everything the property needs. We also take pictures while we are there and attach copies to the form. Sometimes a deal will fall apart and six months later you'll get a call and the deal is resurrected. With pictures and a completed form, you can recall the deal without driving back to the property. We also use this form in our short-sale package.

CHAPTER 6

How to Approach the Bank

To really understand short-sales it is imperative that you understand where the bank representatives are coming from. In the past, the typical bank rep had 30 to 50 short-sale files at any given time. A few years ago that number went to 300 to 500 at any given time. Currently, because of the crazy foreclosure market, some reps may have as many as 700 files—or more! Imagine how stressed out you would be if you had 700 files on your desk and someone called and asked, "Do you...um...do...uh...short-sales?"

Sounding like you know what you are doing can make or break a deal. Does anyone know it is your first deal besides you? No way, so act like a pro even if you aren't yet. With our help, you'll be a pro in no time.

Upon initial contact, the bank will ask for an "Authorization to Release Information" form mentioned in the previous chapter. Due to privacy laws, the bank rep cannot disclose personal information pertaining to the homeowners without their written consent.

To obtain this information, you must have the borrowers (your sellers, the homeowners) sign what's called an authorization to release form. This form states the borrower's name, loan number, Social Security number, lender name, and contact information. It also gives the lender permission to speak to persons named on the form. Don't waste your time contacting a lender without this form. Have it ready to fax to the lender as soon as you make contact. Get the fax number and the right person to speak with and get busy. Note that some lenders require the form to be notarized, and some lenders have their own form they want signed by the borrower.

How to Get the Bank Interested in Talking to You

When you contact a bank about a short-sale, it's because the homeowner is either behind in payments or in foreclosure. When that happens to homeowners, the bank usually sends them a letter explaining their options. One of the options listed is a short-sale, even though most homeowners don't understand what a short sale is.

At first contact with the bank and after submitting the authorization to release form, you will explain to the loss mitigation representative that not only is the property in question owned by someone in financial distress, but in addition, the property needs work (if that's the case), the property values have dropped (if that's the case), and no one else is interested in buying this property but you.

Obviously, you will continue to share how these factors affect your offer, so you'll ask where you can fax the short-sale offer and to whom. The bank representative will tell you exactly what forms the bank needs in order to make a decision on accepting the short-sale. Anytime you can include more documentation than they ask for to help justify your offer, do it.

What the Bank Wants from an Investor

The number one thing the banks want from you is confidence that you will close on the deal. We typically begin the conversation by stating that we are full-time investors, we do short-sales for a living, we have a package ready for 123 Elm Street, and we'd like to know where we need to be in terms of price to close this deal.

The bank will usually ask for only a few documents from the homeowner—typically the purchase contract, estimated closing costs (net sheet), and hardship letter. This isn't nearly enough ammunition to justify any offer that would be substantially below the mortgage balance. That's why we teach you to submit a package worth its weight in gold.

Later in this chapter, you'll see the sample script we use when speaking to the bank. Practice it a few times before you call the bank, and you will sound like you have been doing this for years!

How to Get Through to a Stonewalling Lender

There are a few hurdles we want to help you overcome when you get involved in short-sales.

Trying to get through to the right person is difficult at times. Getting that individual to actually answer their phone is even more difficult. That's why it's important to get the fax number or e-mail address of the person you will be working with. Many times, their voice mail will tell you not to leave a message more than once in any 24-hour period. That's how inundated they are. The trick is to do your best to get the rep's e-mail address.

E-mail is one of the best ways for them to communicate with you. But if you can't get an e-mail address and phone tag doesn't work, then fax them repeatedly until you are contacted. They have so many delinquent loans they are dealing with that files are often pushed to the bottom of the pile. Constant communication helps keep your short-sale on the top of the pile. We don't want you to be so pushy that the rep doesn't like you, but be professionally persistent enough to be taken seriously, even though you are a pain. Have you ever heard that the squeaky wheel gets the oil?

We have faxed the same rep over 200 times in one day ... seriously. On one particular day, a rep simply refused to call us back. We had left over 13 messages. We were both very frustrated and were at our wits' end. We don't know what came over us, but we decided to fax until we got a call back. We began faxing throughout the day. Finally, at the end of the day, the rep called, yelling, "You faxed me over 200 times today! What is wrong with you?!" We stated that we hadn't received a confirmation and didn't realize how many times the fax had gone through. The rep stated that she would never work with us, because we had gotten her in trouble. We reminded her that tomorrow was a new day and we had nothing to do tomorrow except fax her again, and, after a long pause, she took our deal. It was great!

Presenting Your Short-Sale Offer to the Bank

The key to success is to pin the rep down as to when you can expect an answer. If you are dealing with a bank for the first time, you may want to call the loss mitigation department to confirm that the bank accepts short-sales before you spend time preparing the entire package.

All of the larger banks do short-sales:

> ➤ Washington Mutual.

> ➤ Bank of America.

> ➤ Wells Fargo.

> ➤ Countrywide Bank.

> ➤ First Union.

> ➤ Option One Mortgage Corporation.

> ➤ Ocwen Financial Corporation.

> ➤ First Franklin.

> ➤ Litton Loan Servicing.

There are many more. The problem with calling the bank first is that you may get a new person who has no idea what a short-sale is and tells you no when, in fact, the bank does do short-sales. We prefer to prepare the package, call loss mitigation, and ask who we need to fax the package to in order to get our deal accepted. We assume that all banks will say yes.

> ➤ Most banks do say yes to some sort of a short-sale. If you have a property worth $100,000 with a $100,000 mortgage balance, and the bank accepts $90,000, the bank considers that a short-sale. It's just not a short-sale we would accept.

> ➤ If the bank does not have a loss mitigation department, ask for the foreclosure department, workout department, loan modification department, late payment department, bankruptcy, or whoever helps homeowners in distress.

Give the seller's name and loan number and ask for the representative who is handling the seller's account. Once you have the right person on the line, ask for the fax number and fax the authorization to release form while you are on the phone with the rep.

Before you begin dealing with the loss mitigation reps, it is important you understand the mind-set of this person. Most of these folks are overworked and underpaid. Remember, some have as many as 700 files on their desk at any given time. Because these reps are so overwhelmed with their case loads, they often blow you off on the phone if you don't appear to know what you are doing.

There are several ways to represent yourself to loss mitigation:

> *As a friend.* You could represent yourself as a friend trying to help. The problem with this approach is that the rep may think you have no experience and may not want to bother with you. On the positive side, the bank may like the fact that you are not a smooth-talking investor.

> *As an investor.* The rep may think that as an investor you are out to take advantage of the homeowners as well as make a killing from the bank's loss. On the positive side, the rep will like the fact that you have experience and will be less trouble than someone with no experience. With bank reps having as many properties to unload as they currently have, presenting yourself as an investor is a really good thing. The reps know that you have experience, that they won't have to train you, and that you will make their hectic job easy.

> *As a real estate agent (if you have a license).* The bank realizes that as an agent you are a neutral third party, but the bank may not have the confidence that you will follow through without a buyer, because agents show houses, not purchase them. On the positive side, the bank may take your offer more seriously because you are an agent and are considered a professional.

You have to decide which role best suits you. We have been able to use all three with great success. There is no right or wrong way to present yourself. The key is to let the rep know that you are easy to work with and will make the transaction as smooth as possible.

When speaking with the loss mitigation representative, always be professional and refer to the sellers by their first names as often as possible. Bring as much emotion into the conversation with the rep as possible in the hope that this will help the rep's decision to accept a short-sale become more meaningful rather than solely financial.

Your initial conversation with the loss mitigation representative will go something like this:

YOU: Hello, Mary, my name is John and I am working with **Bob and Sally Brown** to help them with their situation. May I have your fax number so I can send you my authorization to release?

BANK: Sure, my fax is 555-456-7890.

YOU: Hold on, I'll send it right now. *(Fax it while you have the rep on the phone.)*

BANK: Okay, I've received it. How can I help you?

YOU: As you know, **Bob and Sally** are in foreclosure. I told them I would do my best to help them if I could. Upon researching the property it looks as if they owe more than it's worth. **Bob** thinks their mortgage balance is $100,000. Is that correct?

BANK: Yes, it is.

YOU: Great! When is the property set for the sheriff's sale? My real estate agent says the property is worth only about $40,000 to $50,000 because it needs so much work. Based on the fact that **Bob and Sally** owe far more than their property is worth, I'm willing to purchase the property, but only if you can take a short-sale. Where do we need to be pricewise to get this deal closed?

BANK: Fax a sales contract and a net sheet and we'll see what we can do.

YOU: Great, Mary. I will have that faxed to you as soon as possible. I'd like you to know that **I am prepared to close quickly** and will not make you work hard on this deal only to bail out at the end. I can close as soon as you can get me a yes.

BANK: Fine.

YOU: I'd like to ask you a few questions if I may. Do you make the decisions or does your boss?

BANK: My boss does.

YOU: Great. How often do you meet with your boss?

BANK: I meet with my boss twice a month.

YOU: Great. When was the last time you met with your boss?

BANK: We met last week.

YOU: So ... if I get you everything you need today, will you be able to present my offer to your boss next week?

BANK: Yes, if you get the information I need I'll present your offer next week.

YOU: Okay, great. I'll get you as much information as I can by the end of the day. Then I'll call you to see if my offer is in a range that your bank can accept. What percentage does your bank usually discount?

BANK: It's different with every deal. Get your offer to me and we'll discuss it then.

YOU: One last thing: I just want to remind you that **I can close quickly.** I am sending you a cover letter, a sales contract, a hardship letter from the homeowners, a list of repairs, a net sheet, and pictures. Is there anything else your bank requires?

BANK: Wow, it sounds like you have a great package ready. That will be plenty of information to get started. Get your package to me and I'll do my best.

YOU: Great, I'll stay in touch.

See how often we use the homeowner's names? We also reassured the rep that we could close quickly. We also told the rep what we were sending and asked if there were any other items the bank required. This shows your professionalism and experience.

Once your package is submitted, follow up until you get a yes.

The Asset Manager's Role

Something that most investors don't realize is that the loss mitigation rep is not the end of the line in the short-sale process. The loss mitigators present the offers to their bosses, who in turn, present the offers to *their* bosses. The loss mitigator's boss is called an asset manager.

When a loan is granted, properties are placed in a larger portfolio. This portfolio may have 2,000 loans in it. The managers/investors/accountants assigned to a particular portfolio have the final say on a short-sale.

Here is an example of how portfolios work: Suppose you borrowed money from Bank of America to buy your house. Several months after your purchase, you receive a letter telling you to make your payments to a different bank from now on. That is because Bank of America sold a group of property-collateralized notes—a portfolio—to another bank, which now holds your loan. Several years may pass, and the second bank sends you a letter telling you to pay still a different bank, and this continues for the life of the loan. These loans are being sold and serviced by other banks or investors, who make money on the spread, yield, and interest.

The same holds true with a short-sale. Each property is part of a larger portfolio, and the loss mitigator's boss—the asset manager—has access to someone representing that portfolio. The portfolio representative has the final say. Most of the asset managers have guidelines that they must work within. Maybe the asset manager is allowed to discount up to 70 percent of the retail value of the property, but must present all offers, even those lower than that, to the portfolio representative. The portfolio rep could be an investor, an accountant, a hedge fund manager, or anyone placed in charge. This position can be held by various people. Portfolios can be different sizes as well. One portfolio may contain 2,000 property-collateralized notes, while another has only 500. Most banks will not sell an individual note from a portfolio unless it is a defaulting note. This is why short-sales can be difficult at times—based on the group this particular loan is in, you may get different answers from the same bank!

One of our students was working on two short-sales in Detroit. Both houses were on the same street; in fact, they were side by side. Both loans were with Washington Mutual, and our student was working with the same loss mitigation rep on both properties. The loss mitigation rep presented the offers to the asset manager. The asset manager then proceeded to present the two offers to the portfolio investors; he got a yes on one and a no on the other. Each property was in a different portfolio with different guidelines as to how to settle losses. Imagine . . . the same bank, two houses side by side, and the same loss mitigation rep—anyone would expect the same answer for both properties. It's enough to make you crazy.

Working with the Portfolio Representative Directly

We hate to be the bearer of bad news, but you will never be able to work with the portfolio rep directly. Remember, the portfolio may contain 2,000 properties. No portfolio rep is going to deal with each property individually. That is why they have an asset manager, to field the deals and call only when necessary.

Many investors want to present their offers directly to the asset manager, but this is not the way it works, either. A typical loss mitigation department may have 500 reps (gatekeepers), who in turn have access to five asset managers. The asset managers typically will not work directly with real estate investors, because they want us to go through proper protocol. If a deal gets tough, sometimes we do try to go over the head of the gatekeeper and go directly to the asset manager, but this does not build a long-lasting relationship with our rep.

Our goal in every short-sale is to build long-lasting relationships with the loss mitigation reps so that they will say yes next time with less hassle. Once you build a relationship with a rep, you can often simply call and present a verbal offer. This is when short-sales get really fun and easy!

Getting Your Short-Sale Assigned to a Loss Mitigation Rep

With foreclosures being rampant, many loss mitigation offices are understaffed. In the past, as soon as a few payments were missed, a loss mitigation rep was assigned. Because of understaffing, it may take a month or two to get your deal assigned to a rep. While we don't want this to discourage you, we do want to be honest. As long as there is time before the sheriff's sale, this should not present a problem.

We can't say it enough: Have several deals in the works at *all* times. This way, if it takes a few weeks to get one deal assigned, you have others on which you can make progress. Part of building a successful business is to be able to duplicate what you are doing. Keeping several deals in the works will allow you to become very successful.

Because there are several states with *very* short foreclosure processes (Virginia, Georgia, Texas, and a few others), waiting for a rep to be assigned can prove challenging. The good news is that there are a few things you can do if there isn't much time before the sale date.

As our first option, we ask the bank rep to postpone the sale. Surprisingly, the banks will often do this. Remember, banks are in the business of lending money, not owning property. Also, with the huge number of properties in or near foreclosure, banks don't want to risk getting stuck with a property if they can unload it to you. We typically ask for a 30-day postponement in order for us to complete the short-sale. If you need longer than 30 days, ask for it up front. Once the banks say yes, they want you to close, so do not ask for more time at that point.

If asking for a postponement does not work, offer to pay the attorney's fees to postpone the sale. Typically, the bank will take a small fee to postpone the sale. If this option is used, the home-owners must come up with the funds for the fee. If you pay for the postponement and the deal does not close, you have no way to get your money back; the bank keeps the money because it postponed the sale. Surprisingly, most homeowners are able to get their hands on some cash. Remember, they haven't been making mortgage pay-ments for a while and may have some cash saved.

If these options don't work, the homeowners can always file for bankruptcy, which we will discuss later.

Your offer is submitted; you used your scripts to build a good relationship with the loss mitigation rep. Now let's look at some additional items the bank may ask for.

Additional Information the Bank May Require

As you can see in the conversation with the bank, the bank usually asks for just a net sheet and a sales contract. Just sending those two items does not build a strong enough case, and that is why you send our complete short-sale package. Sometimes the bank will ask for additional information before considering your offer. It doesn't happen often, but we want you to be aware in case it happens to you.

When the bank asks for additional information, it is to appease shareholders. Every property you will negotiate to buy has a mort-gage that is part of a larger package.

Each of these packages has investors or shareholders who make the final decision as to whether to accept a short-sale. Some shareholders will okay a short-sale; some will not. When your loss mitigation rep asks for more information, it is to show the shareholders why they should accept your offer.

With luck and persistence, you should get about 60 to 70 percent of your offers accepted. Almost every bank will accept a short-sale; the key is getting it low enough to make it a good deal for you.

Let's discuss some additional items you may need to produce.

Hardship Package

Some banks require what they call a hardship package. This is a package the bank will send via mail or fax to you or to the homeowners to be completed by the borrower (the homeowner, not you). The bank's hardship package looks like a loan application. The bank is trying to determine that the homeowners really have no money and are not just choosing to walk away from the property.

The homeowners will have to include W-2s, bank statements, paycheck stubs, and a financial statement.

The bank is much more inclined to accept a short-sale if a real hardship is proven. Keeping in mind this fact, the seller should complete the package accordingly.

Some of these items will not exist, but put together what you can. If there are required items missing, simply take a blank sheet of paper and type at the top of it the name of the missing item and then the words, "There are no ... because ..."

For example:

➤ Paycheck Stubs: "There are no paycheck stubs because we are currently unemployed."

➤ Tax Returns: "There are no tax returns because we haven't had the money to file for two years" or "... because we have been unemployed for over a year."

Make sure each sheet you create is signed by the homeowners. You may have to help the homeowners complete the hardship package. The hardship package can often seem overwhelming.

When you speak with the bank about the short-sale, *make yourself the contact person*. This way, the bank will fax the hardship package to you. You can then get it to the sellers to be completed.

TIP: Whenever you work with a bank that requires a hardship package, make and keep a copy of that package for future reference.

The next time you work with another seller who has a mortgage with that same bank, you will be able to get the package completed during the first appointment. This will help expedite the short-sale process, because you never know when you will get another opportunity to sit down with the homeowners or to speak with the loss mitigation rep.

Listing Agreement

Sometimes the bank will ask for a real estate listing agreement as part of its requirements for accepting a short-sale. The listing agreement proves that the homeowners were or are trying to sell the property. The bank wants to be sure that your offer isn't the only offer that has been presented.

Your team-player agent can list the property for the homeowners and provide the listing agreement for the bank. Once the property is entered into the Multiple Listing Service (MLS), your agent should be able to mark the property "pending" due to the fact that you have a fully signed sales agreement.

When determining the asking price for the listing agreement, the typical agent will add the mortgage balance, the real estate commission, and the proceeds for the homeowners. Unfortunately, that will make the asking price unrealistic, which is why it hasn't sold in the first place. Real estate agents who list properties too high do nothing but hurt the homeowners. We can't tell you how many times we have seen properties listed for much higher than retail sit on the market and then be sold at the sheriff's sale. The poor homeowners put all their eggs in the real estate agent's basket and lost.

TIP: It's important for you to know that banks that seek a listing agreement will typically pay the real estate commission.

When looking for a real estate agent to assist you in a case where a listing agreement is required, confirm that the bank pays the commission. If so, this is a win-win situation for the real estate agent, because you complete the short-sale and the bank will pay the agent a commission.

> ➤ Find a real estate agent who understands what you are doing and realizes you are here to help, not hurt, the homeowners.
> ➤ If the homeowners have been trying to sell the property themselves, ask the bank whether a copy of the newspaper ad (or whatever proof they have) will suffice.

If the bank requires a listing agreement, ask the rep whether you can close now—or do you have to wait until the listing agreement expires? Typically, when the bank wants a listing agreement, it wants a 90-day agreement. If you must wait until the agreement runs its course, you'll be waiting 90 days.

FYI: Federal Housing Administration (FHA) and Department of Veterans Affairs (VA) loans require 90 days on the market.

We always ask the bank if the property actually needs to be listed—or will a copy of the listing agreement suffice? Often, the bank will accept a copy for the file and forgo the time frame on the listing agreement.

Again, it goes back to satisfying the bank's checklist. A copy may satisfy the checklist and you are back in business!

I found a house worth $70,000 that was in good condition. I was able to buy it for $30,000. I wholesaled it to a rehabber for $45,000 and made $15,000. The best part is, I never took ownership of the property! It was just like Dwan said fast and easy! Thanks!

Ray J., Georgia

Proof of Funds/Preapproval Letter

Your offer is always taken more seriously when you back it up with funds! This is a letter that shows you have financing in place and are able to close on the contract. A mortgage broker can prepare a prequalification letter for you if you are obtaining bank financing, or you can get a proof of funds letter from any hard-money lender.

Hard-money lenders are private individuals or privately owned companies that lend their own money against property based on the equity in the property. Their loans are high-rate, interest-only, short-term balloon mortgages.

However, compared to similar bank mortgages, hard-money loans are a much better deal. These lenders can close quickly, have very minimal loan requirements, and don't care about the condition of the property.

FYI: If you are planning to wholesale the property because you have no cash, don't worry about a proof of funds letter. The rehabber you are wholesaling the property to can provide a proof of funds letter from the person lending the money to the rehabber.

If you have the cash to close the deal, you can use a bank statement or letter from your bank stating that the funds are available. Be certain to state the amount available in your letter as equal to the amount being offered or slightly less. If you have more, great! Now is not the time to show off. If you have more and show it, the bank is more likely to counter your offer with an increased amount coincidentally similar to the amount on your bank statement.

Your proof of funds letter should look similar to the one shown in Figure 6.1.

Most of the time, the bank will accept the short-sale package you submit. If the bank does ask for these additional items, submit them as soon as possible. Time is always of the essence when working on a short-sale. Your homeowners are usually trying to beat the sheriff's sale and will be on pins and needles.

FIGURE 6.1   Proof of Funds Letter

June 18th

Sterling Mortgage

182 Barns Avenue

Allentown, Pa 43987

Re: Proof of Funds

To Whom It May Concern:

Lender has inspected the property located at 893 Smith Street and has approved Dwan for a $350,000 loan. This commitment is good for 45 days from today.

Cordially,

Signed by Your Lender

My Offer Is Submitted—Now What?

Once you have submitted your offer to the bank, it is just a matter of time. Be sure to follow up with the bank every few days. You can leave phone messages, as well as faxing or e-mailing.

There is nothing more frustrating that waiting for the loss mitigation rep to call you back with a yes, no, or counteroffer. We like to pin down the rep as to when we can expect an answer.

Here are a few "first conversation" tips for getting a quicker response:

YOU: Do you make the decision?

BANK: No.

YOU: Who does?

BANK: My boss.

YOU: May I present my offer to your boss?

BANK: Our company doesn't allow it.

YOU: How often do you meet with your boss?

BANK: Every two weeks.

YOU: Great—when did you meet last?

BANK: We met last week.

YOU: So you won't be meeting with your boss for another week, correct?

BANK: That's right.

YOU: So if I have a completed package to you and the BPO [broker price opinion] is done before next week, is there any reason you can't give me an answer next week when you meet with your boss?

BANK: I don't see why not.

YOU: Let me ask you another quick question. Let's say you meet with your boss next week and he counteroffers. Do I have to wait another two weeks for another answer or, at that point, can you present another offer immediately?

BANK: I can present offers only every two weeks.

YOU: Okay, then, I'm going to get you everything you need. When I do, will you really go to bat for me? Bob and Sally are so depressed and I really need you to help me to help them. Can I really count on you?

BANK: Absolutely. I want to get this deal off my desk as much as you want to get the short-sale accepted. I'll do whatever I can to get the deal done.

YOU: Great, you'll have everything you need tomorrow.

We need to know going in when we can expect an answer. The key is to pin down the rep. With this conversation, we know it may take as long as four weeks to get an answer. This being the case, we'll be working on several deals at a time. We don't want to wait four weeks only to receive a no and have no other deals in the works.

It's important for you to understand that loss mitigation reps have different ways they present their offers to the asset manager. Unfortunately, there is no method set in stone.

> Some banks have an open door policy, which means your rep can present an offer at any time.

> Other reps meet with a board or panel on a weekly, monthly, or bimonthly basis.

> Still other reps may have a specific time set aside daily, weekly, or even monthly.

Whatever the way, ask questions so you know what to expect.

We've had students tell us that they spent three months on one short-sale. Our question is always ... why? The problem is that the students did not pin down the rep as to when the rep meets with the asset manager and when they could expect an answer. Once you have this information, your deals will happen much faster. If they do take longer, you'll know to expect that going in.

One of several things will happen as a result of your offer: The bank may say yes right off the bat, the bank may counteroffer, or the bank may say no without further explanation. When the bank says no without explanation, try to pry the reason out of the rep. In many cases, the offer was just too low and the bank could not entertain it because it was not in the acceptable range.

For example, you may have offered $142,500 and the offer needed to be at least $150,000 for the bank to entertain it. When this happens, offer the minimum amount that the bank suggested (i.e., $150,000), and wait for the bank to counter or accept.

TIP: Know when the sheriff's sale is. If the homeowners are set to lose their property in two weeks and the rep just informed you that a decision can't be made for three weeks, the house will sell before a decision can be reached.

We'll talk about how to handle this a little later in the book (see Chapter 9 on buying more time).

CHAPTER 7

Negotiating with a Second or Third Mortgage Holder

When there are second, third, or further mortgages against the property, you must negotiate with each of their holders separately for a short-sale.

Keep in mind that sometimes you will negotiate only with inferior lien holders because the first mortgage is in a good loan to value (LTV) position and the lender will not accept a short-sale. Your deal then hinges on the second mortgage holder accepting a short-sale, since the first mortgage balance is low to begin with relative to the property's value.

One of the best short-sale strategies to use with inferior lien holders is to let them know that the first will not entertain a short-sale offer unless the second receives zero!

This is true with many first mortgage holders. Seconds are aware of this policy and will usually take deep discounts.

The same short-sale steps will apply, with only a few important differences. The differences are:

➤ Ask for the decision maker.

➤ Send the same short-sale package, but *without* the sales contract and net sheet.

➤ Send a letter of intent in place of the sales contract.

➤ The inferior lien holders do not need a net sheet because what you offer is exactly what they get.

➤ Write a different cover letter stating the fact that the inferior lien holder will be wiped out at the sale.

➤ Have the homeowners write a separate hardship letter stating the fact that the lien holder will be wiped out.

➤ Deal with each lien holder separately.

Before we get into the conversation with the second lender, take a look at this amazing short-sale. The second lien holder took a *huge* discount. After that, we'll look at the adjusted letters you'll need to submit.

Hi Dwan and Sharon,

I wanted to share our story of the best short-sale we've completed. It started in around August of 2006 and closed in May of 2007. We resold it within three weeks of the purchase.

I was on the road down in Fort Lauderdale when my wife called me insisting that I had to drive over and meet a client at her bank. She told me she had just met this client on the phone as a referral and the woman wanted to quitclaim deed her house to us! I'm not that smart, but when someone wants to give me a house, the least I can do is listen to what she has to say! So off I went to the local bank branch to meet the homeowner.

It turned out that Margaret, the homeowner, had allowed a friend to buy a house using her name in February 2005. It was a really nice-looking waterfront four-bedroom, two-bathroom home in a gated community. Her friend told her that if she would buy the house for her, she and her husband would move in and make all the payments. Unfortunately, Margaret agreed. Margaret is a 32-year-old housekeeper earning $2,000 per month who rents a spare bedroom to live in. She had given power of attorney to her friend and had no idea she was being qualified for a $400,000 stated income, stated assets (SISA) loan.

Well, the marriage fell apart less than six months later; hubby moved out, and without hubby's income, the friend abandoned the house (without telling Margaret, I might add). So Margaret needed help in a big way. She found out about the situation when she was served with foreclosure papers. In any event, Margaret agreed to work with us and signed a purchase agreement, "Authorization to Release Information" forms for both the first and second mortgage holders, and a quitclaim deed to the property. All she wanted was her credit salvaged.

Well, two weeks later, Margaret, my wife, and I decided to take a road trip together and go see the house. It took about two and a half hours (and two speeding tickets) to get there, but it was well worth it. As we pulled up to the house, Margaret started crying. The place was beautiful. Then we went in. By the time we got there, the house had been vacant for at least eight months. The wood floors had buckled because of the high humidity, and mold was everywhere. The kitchen and bathroom cabinets were destroyed; one kitchen wall and two bedroom walls were fuzzed with mold. The pool was a beautiful dark green. It smelled like money! We took lots of photos, did a property inspection report, installed a lockbox, and drove back to Boca Raton.

We used Sharon and Dwan's hardship letter examples to help Margaret write her hardship letter, obtained comparable sales of the property, and started to put together our first offer to the lenders. Fort Myers, as it turned out, had been one of the fastest appreciating markets in the country. But once the hurricane hit, values started to slide and it became one of the fastest areas to depreciate. The property was purchased in 2005 for $400,000, and by September 2006 homes were selling for $350,000 and values were falling at over 2 percent per month. We also called several mold specialists for remediation estimates. Some wanted over $1,000 to do an air quality report and remediation estimate! We settled on a firm that gave us a fair price, and its remediation estimate came in at over $110,000! That was exactly what we needed as support for our photos.

Following the plan in Dwan's short-sale course, our initial offer focused on the homeowner's situation and the condition of the house. We offered $30,000 ($29,000 to the first mortgage holder and $1,000 to the second). We flooded both lenders with *information and supporting documentation, insisting they take our offers seriously.*

They ordered interior BPOs [broker price opinions], and when the BPO agents called, we told them the house was full of mold and the remediation company did repair estimates wearing space suits. They said, "Thanks but no thanks; we'll tell the lender that we'll pass on this one." This happened several times over the next few months, but for some reason the foreclosure case hadn't progressed.

So by February 2007, we decided to have the mold guy take another look at the property to confirm that his estimate was still good. On the bank representative's recommendation, we jumped our second offer to $140,000 to get closer to what the bank wanted. But this time, at the suggestion of a very helpful loss mitigation representative at GMAC, we had an appraisal done on the property and included the same repair estimate that justified our $140,000 offer. We also sent in several copies of newspaper articles printed off the Internet showing the condition of the Fort Myers housing market (per the course) and a spreadsheet outlining GMAC's expected holding costs if it took the property back (also per the course).

Fortunately, at this point, GMAC was hamstrung. A foreclosure sale date had been set for May 2, and it was now the beginning of April. They countered our offer at $155,000. We countered back at $145,750 with only $750 going to the second mortgage. Finally GMAC agreed to the short-sale. They had discounted a $320,000 first mortgage to a net of $145,000. They also agreed to waive the deficiency judgment.

Now it was on to the second mortgage holder. They had been ignoring us for all these months, but now there was a foreclosure sale date. The first thing their loss mitigation representative told me was, "Don't think for a moment that we're gonna discount this loan down to $1,500 or $2,500. It's gonna take at least $25,000 for us to settle." So using the communication skills I learned from

Bill Twyford (Dwan's Husband), I said I absolutely understood. Then I explained the property situation to him and said that there was an agreed settlement from the first mortgage for only $145,750. Needless to say, he was not very happy. He told me to resubmit everything to him—photographs, appraisal, and so on. A week later the second mortgage loss mitigation representative called me back and asked if I thought I could get him at least $1,000! Instead of saying yes right away, I told him that the decision wasn't my call, but I'd check and get back to him. He then approved the $750 offer on a principal mortgage balance of $80,000!

I had hard-money financing lined up to close, and the lender gave me $200,000 based on a $320,000 value. Margaret was ecstatic. The foreclosure sale date was right around the corner and the closing was set two days before that sale date. After paying closing costs, delinquent real estate taxes, and HOA [homeowners association] fees, we walked away from the closing table with just over $34,000 in our pocket because we borrowed more than we paid.

In the meantime, my wife had discovered that there was a REIA group in Fort Myers that had an online forum. She was writing back and forth with several rehabbers who were interested in the home, and within less than a week of ownership, I drove over to meet one of them.

Fully expecting that I was going to end up renting an apartment and starting a remodeling project on the other side of the state, I told the buyer that he had to pay me $230,000 cash. After a day or so, he sent a full-price offer and closed a week and a half later.

We netted nearly $65,000 on that deal and didn't have to make even one mortgage payment. Margaret is in the process of a credit cleanup and is extremely thankful.

Thanks for everything.
David and Elieth Ginsburg

Your Conversation with the Second Lender

Our goal is always to get the second lien holder (or third, etc.) to give us the number they will accept first. If we can't get a figure from them, we move forward with our offer. We offer $1,000 as a starting offer regardless of the amount of the second mortgage. Whether the second is $10,000 or $85,000, we start at $1,000. Remember, you can always go up, rarely down.

We find that when the second mortgage is large (over $50,000), the lien holder will usually accept around 10 percent of the mortgage balance. The smaller seconds usually take $1,000 or so. We've had many $25,000 seconds accept $1,000, and so have our students.

Second mortgage holders know that they will be wiped out at the sheriff's sale; therefore, they usually negotiate. Typically, the second will give you a figure, if not a decision, on the first or second call.

Your conversation with the second will go something like this:

YOU: Hello, Mary, my name is John Smith and I am working with Bob and Sally Brown to help them with their situation. May I have your fax number so I can send you my authorization to release information?

SECOND: Sure, my fax is 555-456-7890.

YOU: Hold on, I'll send it right now. (Fax it while you have the rep on the phone.)

SECOND: Okay, I've received it. How can I help you?

YOU: As you know, Bob and Sally are facing foreclosure and have been trying to sell their home for quite some time. They can no longer afford the home, and the repairs are too extreme for them to fix. They told me that they owe your company $25,000. Are you the person who makes the decision about a short-sale?

SECOND: Yes, I am the person, and we will entertain a short-sale; fax me your offer.

YOU: Okay, Mary, I will have that faxed to you as soon as possible. Can you give me an idea of what you'd be willing to accept?

SECOND: Since they owe $25,000, I believe we would be able to accept $10,000.

YOU: Okay, I believe we may be able to work with that, but I'm not certain. Could you fax that acceptance to me today so I can crunch my numbers to see if that figure works for me?

SECOND: I'll get it to you right away.

Are we going to accept the second's initial offer? No! Let the rep fax you an acceptance letter for the $10,000. You can then call back and state that upon further review you don't believe you can make the numbers work at $10,000.

You are now negotiating down from $10,000, as opposed to negotiating down from the original $25,000.

You are now ready to call again and negotiate further. Your next call will go like this:

YOU: Hi, this is John. I have gone over the numbers several times. I really appreciate your coming down to $10,000; however, that number isn't going to work for me. Upon further review, the property just needs too much work.

SECOND: We think our acceptance of $10,000 is more than fair.

YOU: I totally understand how you feel. Let's review the facts. ... The sale is in 30 days. Because Bob and Sally owe what their property is worth, your second mortgage will be wiped out at the sale. I know that the way a second works is that you have to purchase the first in order to be the winning bidder at the sale. You are a bank and in the business of making money. It does not make financial sense to spend $150,000 just to save your $25,000 mortgage. Isn't it better to receive something instead of nothing?

SECOND: We realize that we will be wiped out. What are you offering?

YOU: After really crunching the numbers, the most I can offer is $1,000. I have to negotiate with the first, arrange a closing, and the property needs to be rehabbed. With all that, $1,000 is the best I can do.

SECOND: I don't think I can get that approved. I'll run it by my boss and let you know.

YOU: Great, make sure to present the complete package (hardship letter, comps, pictures, cover letter from you, proof of hardship, etc.) to your boss. I'm sure he or she will agree once he or she sees what a burden this property would be to your company. I can close as soon as the first gets me an approval letter. I am also sending several letters of recommendation from other banks I have worked with in the past. I want your boss to realize that I am serious and will close on time and get this nightmare off your books.

SECOND: Okay, send them over. I'll let you know in a few hours.

Wait a few hours and proceed:

YOU: This is John. How'd we do?

SECOND: Good news—the boss said yes. I will send you an acceptance letter today. We'll coordinate our closing with the first mortgage. When will you have that date?

YOU: I am thrilled you have agreed to the short-sale. The first wants to close in 30 days. If you can give me until that time, we're good. It has been a pleasure working with you. You're a professional. I'll be certain to send you a letter of recommendation for your file.

SECOND: It's been great working with you as well. I look forward to working with you again in the future.

It's that simple. We have had hundreds of phone calls just like this. As we said, seconds are easy.

If the homeowners have a third or fourth mortgage, have the same conversation. The only difference is that we never offer more than $500. Any lien holder in that position will definitely get wiped out. In some cases, we ask a third or fourth to settle the debt for zero. They often do!

Variations on a Theme

TIP: Sometimes a second mortgage holder will not agree to take less, but will agree to remove the lien from the property and attach it to the homeowners' names unsecured. If this is the only way to put the deal together and the homeowners agree, go for it. The downside to this is that the homeowners still owe a second mortgage on a property they no longer own. Since the loan is now unsecured, the homeowners can file bankruptcy and wipe it out.

When you come across a situation where the first mortgage is low and the second is negotiable, try to purchase the note of the second rather than pursuing a short-sale.

As the new second mortgage holder, you can then take the property "subject to." You simply reinstate the first mortgage, get the deed from the homeowners, and the property is yours.

The sellers must be willing to leave their names on the mortgage for an agreed amount of time in order for this to work.

We use "subject to's" as our main way to collect rentals. The homeowners deed their property to us, we bring the payments current, we continue to make payments for several years, and then we refinance the loan, taking their name off and freeing them to buy something new.

It's a great way to start buying rentals, because you don't have to qualify for the loan. You simply take over someone else's payments, they deed the property to you, and the loan stays in their name. Whoever is on the deed is the owner, not the person on the mortgage.

As you can see, the letters in Figures 7.1 to 7.3 are similar to the cover letter to the first mortgage holder. The only real difference is

FIGURE 7.1   Sample Letter to Junior Lien Holder #1 (Downloadable*)

Dear Mr./Ms. Bank Rep:

This letter serves as our offer of [amount] as payment in full for the above-referenced loan on property located at [address].

As you are aware, Bob and Sally are facing foreclosure and the sale date is coming up soon. I'm sure you've been notified of the foreclosure and **that your lien of [amount] will be wiped out at the sale.**

Due to the extreme hardship Bob and Sally are under as well as the condition of the property, we not only urge you to accept our offer, but **we request that you also waive any deficiency judgment against the homeowners.**

Also attached please find my authorization to release information, hardship letter, comparable sales in the area, photos, and contractor's estimate of repairs.

We are trying to close by the last day of the month and need your assistance to make this deal work.

The homeowners are contemplating bankruptcy, but don't want to go down that path unless they are forced to. They just want to move on with their lives. Their attorney said they could stay in the home free for two years if they file bankruptcy, but they really don't want to do so.

Upon your review of the attachments, please contact us as soon as possible at the letterhead number to discuss your approval.

Thank you for your consideration and prompt attention to this matter.

Sincerely,

[Investor's name]

FIGURE 7.2   Sample Letter to Junior Lien Holder #2 (Downloadable*)

Dear [second mortgage company]:

My name is [name]. I buy notes and defaulting loans all over the United States. I am willing to make an offer on loan #_____ owned by [homeowners' names] on the property located at [address]. **Based on current market prices, the poor condition of the property, and the extensive repairs needed, I am willing to offer [amount] for your second mortgage.**

As I'm sure you know, **your lien of [amount] will be wiped out at the sheriff's sale.** I can close on or before [date].

I also ask that you waive any deficiency judgment against [homeowners' names]. Their attorney wants them to file **Chapter 13** and stall the foreclosure sale. They would rather move on.

Please get back to me ASAP so I can proceed.

Sincerely,

[Investor's name]

*Copyright © 2008 by Dwan Bent-Twyford and Sharon Restrepo. To download and customize this form for your personal use, please visit www.theieu.com/shortsaleform.

that we are letting the second know that we know that they will be wiped out at the sale.

As we mentioned earlier, seconds are usually very willing to short-sale.

As part of the short-sale with the first mortgage, you include a hardship letter. We also send basically the same hardship letter to all the junior lien holders, but we also let them know that their liens will be wiped out.

You don't have to do this step, but we believe it helps.

FIGURE 7.3   Sample Letter to Junior Lien Holder #3 (Downloadable*)

Dear [second, third, or fourth mortgage company]:

My name is [name]. I am working with [homeowners' names] on the situation with their property located at [address].

I understand your outstanding loan is [amount] and will be wiped out at the upcoming sheriff's sale. Based on current market values, the poor condition of the property, the code violations, and the extensive repairs needed, the property is worth far less than the mortgage balances. Therefore, I am willing to buy your mortgage for [amount] as payment in full.

I will close within [amount of time] of your acceptance of this offer. I feel this is a very fair offer based on the poor condition of the property. I hope we can work together. **I am also asking that you waive any deficiency judgment against the homeowners.**

Please get back to me ASAP so I can proceed. Thanks!

Sincerely,

[Investor's name]

*Copyright © 2008 by Dwan Bent-Twyford and Sharon Restrepo. To download and customize this form for your personal use, please visit www.theieu.com/shortsaleform.

If you want to use the same hardship letter that you gave to the first, feel free. We like to deal with each lender independently and use a different letter for each.

An example of a second's hardship letter is shown in Figure 7.4.

The second lien holder is also a banking institution. This is why we try to bring some emotion into the situation.

➤ We back up our offer the same way we do with a first.
➤ We mention bankruptcy in our cover letter as well as the hardship letter.

FIGURE 7.4   Sample Hardship Letter from Distressed Homeowner (Downloadable*)

[Date]

Dear [Second Mortgage Company]:

I am writing this letter to share some of the hardships I have endured over the past year. My property located at [address] is currently facing foreclosure. **In fact, the sale date is set for [day and date].** I have absolutely no way to pay the back payments owed on the first or the second mortgage. **I have had the property listed with a real estate agent for months and have gotten only one serious offer because of the condition of the property.**

Based on the offer I have, I can **pay you** only **[amount] as payment in full.** Please accept this as payment in full; otherwise, I have no other choice but to let the property go to the courthouse sale. **From my understanding, the sale will wipe out your [amount] second mortgage completely,** leaving the first mortgage holder with the property and me with a foreclosure on my credit report. I hope we can somehow avoid this.

I am enclosing my bank statement from [most recent month], late notices on my car, and anything else I can find that will help you to see the financial trouble I am facing. I have also enclosed my tax returns.

I am in the [name of] business and things have been VERY slow over the summer. I am currently looking for another field in which to work. So far, I haven't had much success. I am two months behind on my car, electric, and phone bills, and many, many months behind on the mortgage.

My attorney wants me to **file bankruptcy and said I could live in the house free for 18 months.** I really don't want to do this. I hate to ruin my credit more than it already is.

Please waive any deficiency judgments against me. I have enough problems in my life without owing more money down the road. If there is any other information you need, please feel free to call me.

Sincerely,

[Name of distressed homeowner]

As you now know, bankruptcy will make the foreclosure process drag on for months or even years. In the end, junior lien holders get wiped out unless there is sufficient equity in the property due to a low first mortgage balance. In that case, the second would then receive any funds received over and above the judgment amount of the first.

CHAPTER 8

Key Elements of the Legal Process You Must Understand

T his chapter is designed to familiarize you with the different foreclosure processes, types of liens, and types of mortgages.

It's very important to fully understand the entire foreclosure process and how it works. You cannot be helpful to others if you don't understand the process yourself. Many investors think this business is just about finding good deals. If you understand the legal process and lien priorities, you can turn so-so deals into great deals. Knowledge is a powerful weapon. Use it.

Foreclosure laws can vary greatly state to state. In addition, laws are always changing. It seems that with the crashing market, new laws are being passed every day. Currently, homeowners can refinance their adjustable-rate loans into fixed-rate loans, the banks cannot pursue a deficiency judgment, and more laws are enacted weekly. Some of these new laws are in place temporarily, while others are permanent.

The best way to stay current with the ever-changing laws is to attend your local REIA meetings. Real Estate Investors Association groups typically meet once a month and are designed to keep you current in the changing markets. Another way is to go to our web site often. As laws change, we put them on the site to help you stay current (www.theieu.com). We also place articles on our site daily for you to use when doing short-sales. One of our staff members spends time every day searching for negative articles about property values and trends to assist you in getting the banks to say yes. The articles are great and will make your job a lot easier.

Understanding Ownership versus Debt

In order to understand how the foreclosure process works, you must understand the difference between ownership and debt. Think of a property as having two sides: one side named ownership, and the other named debt. We will call the ownership side the title side; title to the property is held by the property owner. The mortgage represents the debt side of the property.

If a homeowner stops paying the mortgage, the bank cannot sell the property, because it does not own the title side; the homeowner does. The homeowner remains the owner of the property throughout the entire foreclosure process until foreclosure is complete. The lender must initiate and complete the foreclosure process in order to gain title to the property. Many people mistakenly think that if a property is in foreclosure, they can contact the lender and buy it.

Also, many people have the misconception that if John Doe signs a quitclaim deed giving his interest in the property to his ex-wife, Jane Doe, he is no longer responsible for the mortgage.

For example, John and Jane Doe are married, buy a house jointly, and later file for a divorce.

When they obtained the mortgage to purchase the property, they both signed it, placing them on the ownership side. The lender is on the debt side of the property, having the right to foreclose for nonpayment of the mortgage. The lender has no claim to ownership at this time.

John and Jane are now divorced. John signs a quitclaim deed giving his interest in the title to Jane. He now mistakenly thinks she is fully responsible for the mortgage payments. What he does not realize is that his name remains on the mortgage and he is still responsible for the debt. He signed away any legal claims to ownership of the property, leaving him with 0 percent ownership; however, because his name remains on the mortgage, he is 100 percent responsible for the debt. When two or more individuals sign a mortgage and note, each of them is jointly and **severally liable**.

Severally liable   Legal term meaning that each person who signed the mortgage and note is responsible for the entire repayment as if his or her name is the only signature on the document.

Eight months later, Jane is in foreclosure. The bank will seek payment from both John and Jane. If they are unable to stop the foreclosure, the bank will gain title to the property.

Jane's and John's credit reports will each reflect a foreclosure. One way for John to eliminate his responsibility for the debt during the divorce suit is to approach the bank in an attempt to have his name removed from the mortgage. Based on Jane's credit and her ability to make mortgage payments, the lender may or may not allow this. The alternative is for Jane to refinance the current mortgage balance.

Title to the property is held by the owners. The document giving title is called the deed and is recorded in the courthouse of the county in which the property is located. The deed lists the names of the individuals owning the property. If the owners of the property secured a mortgage in order to purchase it, the mortgage will also be recorded in the courthouse, stating the lender's name and the amount borrowed.

A property can be purchased only with the owners' consent and signatures. The lender is not the owner! Accordingly, if a property in foreclosure is vacant and you cannot find the owners, you must wait until the foreclosure sale at the courthouse to bid on the property, or contact the bank after the sale if the bank wins the bid.

Many times, several liens exist against a property. Each lien is given priority over another by the date of recording. This priority is called a position.

For example, a mortgage given to a borrower to purchase a property on January 8 will be in first position, and the mortgage given on February 10 for home improvements will be in second position, provided both were recorded immediately upon execution. When researching liens against a property, it is common to come across two (or more) mortgages filed against the same property with the same title. To see which mortgage has priority, look at the recording dates. The lien that was filed first will take priority over the other(s). The priority of liens will be most important during a foreclosure proceeding.

Let's assume that a property has three mortgages against it: the first from Bank A for $50,000, the second from Bank B for $15,000, and the third from Bank C for $10,000. In the next few scenarios, we will explain the differences among them.

Assume that the owners of this property have stopped making their mortgage payments to each of the three lenders, and Bank A begins a foreclosure suit. Bank A will notify Banks B and C. Banks B and C will be able to protect their interests by choosing to purchase the mortgage from Bank A and continue the suit or to bid their positions at the time of sale. Because payments, late fees, and attorneys' fees accrue during the time spent foreclosing, the first $50,000 lien might then be $57,000.

At the foreclosure sale, Bank A will bid its position, meaning it will bid up to $57,000 to secure its interest. If no one else bids, the bank will receive possession of the property. The bank now holds legal and equitable title. In other words, the bank is now the owner. Unless Banks B and C bid their positions, they will be "washed out," meaning they will not get paid and their liens will wash away or be wiped out.

If Bank B were to bid its position to save its $15,000 lien, it would have to bid $72,000 ($57,000 + $15,000). If Bank B receives ownership of the property, it will have to pay the $57,000 lien to Bank A; Bank C's lien will be washed out.

Accordingly, Bank C would have to bid $82,000 ($57,000 + $15,000 + $10,000) to protect its interest, receive ownership, and pay off Banks A and B for $72,000. Bank C will then receive title to the property and be able to sell the property and be reimbursed for its lien when the property is sold.

Next, assume that in the same scenario Bank B files the foreclosure suit against the owners. Bank B will notify Bank C; however, Bank A does not have to be notified because it has a priority lien. Bank A will be paid regardless of the outcome of the foreclosure sale. Bank B will bid its position at $15,000 plus any fees, and it will have to satisfy Bank A's lien to receive possession. Bank C will be washed out or bid its position at $25,000 ($15,000 + $10,000), but it will have to satisfy Bank A's lien as well as Bank B's lien to receive possession.

Now, assume that in the same scenario Bank C files the foreclosure suit against the owners. In order for Bank C to protect its position, it must bid its judgment amount and upon possession satisfy Banks A and B.

Liens are protected in the order of priority. For instance, when a lien holder files suit, it must satisfy all liens recorded prior to its lien. The higher the priority of a lien, the better the chance of its being satisfied during a foreclosure suit. This is the reason lien holders prefer to be in first position. Liens ranking lower in priority are called inferior, junior, or subordinate liens.

Please note that you will often hear that "the bank will take the house back." This simply means that it will foreclose. The bank never owned the house to begin with; therefore, it is not taking it *back*.

Foreclosure Process

The foreclosure process will vary in each state depending on whether you are in a mortgage state or a deed of trust state. Most mortgage states use the judicial process, whereas most deed of trust states use the power of sale process. Consult your attorney to see which process is used in your state and how your state's law may vary.

In some states, the banks have the choice to use either foreclosure process. When this happens, the bank chooses the fastest method and takes the property as quickly as possible.

Mortgage State: Judicial Foreclosure

The first step of the foreclosure process begins with the nonpayment of the mortgage or lien by the property owner. Banks and lien holders vary on the amount of time they will allow to pass before they begin the foreclosure process. Typically, banks will let the homeowners slide for about six months before they file the foreclosure suit. Foreclosure is costly and the process is long. Banks are not in the business of owning property; they are in the business of lending money.

Banks will go as long as they can before they start the foreclosure process. Once the process has begun, though, the banks try to get the property in their possession as quickly as possible.

The foreclosure process proceeds according to the following steps:

1. A lis pendens is filed on behalf of the plaintiff (the bank). A lis pendens is a notice of pending litigation. Anyone who acquires an interest in the property is subject to the result of litigation. The plaintiff is the party filing the lawsuit. If other parties have

a claim against the property, they can join the lawsuit. Look in the classified section of your local newspaper or check with your county courthouse to see if it offers a publication giving real estate information. This is a good way to find properties in the beginning stages of foreclosure.

2. Service of process (complaint, lis pendens, copy of instruments) is initiated on behalf of the plaintiff(s). The plaintiff(s) either can hire an attorney to represent them or can file pro se (representing themselves).

3. The defendants are the homeowners and anyone who holds an interest in the property. The plaintiff(s) hire a process server, whose job is to serve notice to the defendants. If the defendants are unable to be served personally, then the plaintiff(s) must place an ad in a newspaper circulating in the county in which the property is located. This is called constructive notice.

4. The defendants have a certain number of days to answer the complaint. An answer is a response to the complaint filed by the defendants that admits or denies the allegations contained in the complaint. If an answer is filed by the defendants, the judge will set a hearing date, at which time the defendants must defend themselves against the foreclosure.

5. If no answer is filed within the required time, the plaintiff(s) may move for a default. This may accelerate the foreclosure process in that the plaintiff(s) can move for a summary final judgment.

6. At the hearing on a motion for summary final judgment, if the court grants the motion, a summary final judgment is entered, and a sale date is set. The summary final judgment indicates the sale date and the judgment amount.

7. The property is sold for cash to the highest bidder on the sale date at the courthouse auction. If you are the highest bidder, you must leave the required deposit in cash or cashier's check at that time and pay the balance by a specified time the same day.

8. The clerk of the court will issue a Certificate of Title to the new owner of the property approximately 10 days following the sale.

Deed of Trust State: Trustee Sale

This method of foreclosure is much simpler than a judicial foreclosure. Most trust deeds have a power of sale clause. This clause gives the holder of the deed, usually a trustee, the right to sell the property at a public auction without filing a lawsuit. Your state may also have a summary procedure that will expedite the process.

Here are the steps of a trustee sale:

1. When the property owner is delinquent on one mortgage payment, the lender can instruct the trustee to file a default.

2. The trustee must then write a letter to the borrower confirming that a payment has not been made.

3. Once the missed payment is confirmed, the trustee sends another letter informing the borrower that the loan has been accelerated and demands payment. A reinstatement clause is usually included in language in the security instrument (the mortgage) and may differ from state to state. This clause gives the borrower the right to reinstate, putting a stop to the foreclosure.

4. If no payment is made by the borrower, the trustee must wait a set amount of time (generally three to four weeks) during which the trustee will advertise the property for sale. At the end of the waiting period, the property is sold at public auction.

Because of the simplicity of this method of foreclosure, it is much less expensive.

Deed of Trust States and Mortgage States

The difference between a mortgage and a deed of trust becomes important in the event of a default, due to the speed at which the foreclosure process can be carried out.

To see which category your state falls into, look at the following lists. Regardless of where you live, the lien holder will use the fastest method possible to foreclose on a defaulted note.

Note: Some of the states listed may use both types of foreclosures. Check with your attorney to see where your state falls.

Mortgage States

Alabama	Maine	North Dakota
Arkansas	Massachusetts	Ohio
Connecticut	Michigan	Oklahoma
Delaware	Minnesota	Pennsylvania
Florida	Montana	Rhode Island
Illinois	Nebraska	South Carolina
Indiana	Nevada	Utah
Iowa	New Hampshire	Vermont
Kansas	New Jersey	Washington
Kentucky	New Mexico	Wisconsin
Louisiana	New York	Wyoming

Deed of Trust States

Alaska	Idaho	Tennesssee
Arizona	Maryland	Texas
California	Mississippi	Virginia
Colorado	North Carolina	Washington, D.C.
Hawaii	Oregon	West Virginia

Security Deed State

Georgia

It is a good idea to gain as much knowledge as possible about the foreclosure process in your state. Ask your attorney about any laws or processes that may be of help to you in your quest for properties.

Types of Liens

Prior to purchasing real estate, you must check to see if any liens exist against the property. If so, be aware of the liens and how they affect the property's title. Have an attorney or title company provide you with an owner's title insurance policy to protect your title to the property.

We always check for liens against the properties we buy. We figure since they are in foreclosure, there is a good chance that there could be a title issue. We bought a property once and, because we were in a hurry, didn't do our due diligence. As it turned out, there was a problem.

It was a small house in a tough area. It was boarded up, needing everything, but it did have a new roof. It was going to be a great rental—a cash cow! This was a case when one of us convinced the other to go forward. Our cow was slaughtered three weeks after closing when we drove over to assess the repairs and the house was gone. That's right—vanished! At first, we thought we were on the wrong street. Then the realization hit: The house was gone. The city had placed a demolition order against the property because of its poor condition, and the bank's closing agent (it was an REO) missed it in the title search. We pulled up and sat in our car with our jaws dropped. After a moment of silence, mourning our loss, we began to laugh. Trying to see the good in all things, we felt blessed that this setback hadn't happened to us when we were brand-new and unable to afford the mistake. This could have bankrupted a new, unprepared investor. We just laughed it off and decided never to talk each other into a deal again.

Now we check for liens no matter what! The following are the six most common types of liens found upon reviewing courthouse records:

1. *Judgment:* The decision of a court of law that allows a judgment to become a lien against the individual being sued.
2. *Certified final judgment:* A judgment completely deciding all pending matters before a court, thus ending the need for further litigation. A money judgment, when certified and recorded, can become a lien on real property owned by the individual being sued.
3. *Tax lien:* (1) A lien for nonpayment of property taxes attaches only to the property upon which the taxes are unpaid. (2) A federal income tax lien may attach to all property of the individual owing the taxes.
4. *Lien:* An encumbrance against property for money, either voluntary or involuntary. All liens are encumbrances, but not all encumbrances are liens.
5. *Lis pendens:* A legal notice recorded to show pending litigation relating to real property. It states that anyone acquiring an

interest in said property, subsequent to the date of the notice, may be bound by the outcome of the litigation.

6. *Mortgage:* (1) To hypothecate (pledge) real property as security for the payment of a debt. The borrower (mortgagor) retains possession and use of the property. (2) The instrument by which real estate is hypothecated as security for the repayment of a loan.

Foreclosable Liens

There are various types of liens, and not all are foreclosable liens in all states. The following are four types of liens that may be foreclosable in your state:

1. *Mortgage.* Mortgage foreclosures occur because the homeowners have failed to make the payments on their mortgages. A mortgage can also be foreclosed if the homeowners have breached any of the clauses found in the mortgage. For example, if clauses state that if the homeowners fail to keep the home in livable condition or they transfer ownership without the consent of the mortgage holder, then the mortgage holder can begin a foreclosure. Any mortgage holder in any position of priority (i.e., second, third, etc.) can foreclose for any of these reasons, provided the clauses exist in the mortgage.

2. *Mechanic's lien.* This is a lien placed against a property because the homeowners failed to pay a contractor or supplier for work, services, or supplies. It is a foreclosable lien when the homeowners used their property as collateral for payment of the work, services, or supplies.

3. *Homeowners association lien.* This is a lien placed against a property for failure to pay such things as maintenance fees, amenity fees, special assessments, and other fees that a homeowner has agreed to pay as a condition of ownership.

4. *Municipal code violations.* These violations against a property may be foreclosable, depending on local codes.

Types of Mortgages and Loans

Various types of mortgages can be used by homeowners to finance the purchase of real estate. Here are seven mortgage types:

1. *Conventional:* A mortgage or deed of trust not obtained under a government-insured program. Conventional loans are made by banks. A qualified buyer can get as much as 95 percent of the loan to value (LTV). Some conventional lenders also charge points as part of the closing costs. Each point is equal to 1 percent of the amount being financed.

2. *Federal Housing Administration (FHA):* A federal agency that insures first mortgages, enabling lenders to lend a very high percentage of the sale price. The FHA usually requires only 3 to 5 percent down, including closing costs. FHA guidelines require the seller to pay a portion of the buyer's closing costs. Until the end of 1988, FHA loans were fully assumable, nonqualifying loans.

3. *Department of Housing and Urban Development (HUD):* A federal department responsible for the major housing programs in the United States. This agency controls the disposition of foreclosed real estate on FHA-insured loans. This is what the term *HUD homes* means. In foreclosure cases on FHA-insured loans, HUD may notify the homeowners that they have the right to a workout program. Provided the homeowners are owner-occupants of the property, HUD can purchase the defaulting loan from the institution holding the mortgage, stop the foreclosure, and work out a payment plan with the homeowners.

4. *Department of Veterans Affairs (VA):* Housing loans given to veterans by banks and guaranteed by the Department of Veterans Affairs, enabling veterans to buy residences with little or no money down. VA guidelines require the seller to pay a portion of the buyer's closing costs. An assumable VA loan can be assumed by a nonveteran. Until the end of 1988, VA-guaranteed loans were fully assumable, nonqualifying loans.

5. *Private:* Loans made by private individuals (for example, hard-money lenders, credit unions, profit sharing companies, etc.). Compared to other lenders, a private mortgage lender will charge a higher interest rate, as well as more points.

6. *Equity/home improvement:* A loan based on the equity in a property. The credit of the borrower is not a major factor.

7. *Second/third mortgage:* A mortgage that ranks after a first mortgage in priority. Properties may have two, three, or more mortgages, deeds of trust, or land contracts as liens at the same time. The recording dates will determine priority, but not necessarily whether they are called a first, second, third, or other lien. For example, regardless of the name of the lien, if a second mortgage is recorded *after* a third mortgage, the second mortgage will be third in priority and the third will be second in priority.

As we mentioned in the Introduction of this book, there are several creative but potentially risky loan programs available to new homeowners. Most of these set people up for failure. Take a minute to review these again.

➤ *Teaser adjustable-rate mortgages.* These loans are popular because they offer a very low initial rate, which later resets and rises. With good credit, initial payments can have an interest rate as low as 1 percent! But people consider only the payment today and whether they can afford it now, and not later. When the payment resets, many homeowners find themselves with a payment they can no longer afford, therefore finding themselves in foreclosure. Teaser loans are risky for people who live on the edge of their means. Many people have good credit, but are cash poor. It only takes one or two high payments to throw them into financial disaster.

➤ *Subprime adjustable-rate mortgages.* These loans are easy to get and don't require much verification, causing many people to apply for them. Typically, people with low or unverifiable income apply for these loans. They are typically adjustable-rate loans, but start with a higher initial interest rate, maybe 6 or 7 percent, adjusting as high as 10 to 13 percent on the first adjustment. As with teaser loans, the new payment can cause homeowners to be upside-down on their payments, again, leading to foreclosure.

➤ *Option adjustable-rate mortgages.* These loans are the worst thing I have seen come down the pike. They give homeowners the choice of making a full or partial payment. Even though homeowners are told that if they make a partial payment the balance will go on the back of their loan, most people don't realize what this actually means. Let's say a homeowner borrows $100,000 and has a mortgage payment of $1,000 with an option to pay a partial payment of $450. Each time the homeowner pays $450, the unpaid balance of $550 goes on the back of the loan raising the mortgage balance. In two years, a homeowner could owe $20,000 more than originally borrowed (unpaid balance, plus interest). At some point, so much is owed against the property, it is virtually impossible to sell.

Never take one of these loans. There are approximately 1,000,000 people in foreclosure and the number is expected to rise to 7,000,000 in the next few years. We believe these loans are the main reason so many people are losing their homes. What was supposed to boost the economy is bankrupting it. If you can't afford the *real* payment, you can't afford it . . . period.

CHAPTER 9

When the Bank Says Yes

When the bank says yes, it will send you an acceptance letter. Get your yes in writing as soon as possible.

There have been several cases where we got a yes, the representative quit or was fired before we got the yes in writing, a new rep stepped in, and our deal fell apart.

Another time, we got a yes in writing, the bank sold the note while we were waiting for the closing, and the new bank didn't want to honor the agreement. We had to get an attorney involved. Bottom line—the deal closed as scheduled.

TIP: The second you get your yes, get it in writing. We can't stress this point enough!

A yes is contingent on a few conditions, meaning that the bank will take the deal if you meet its terms. Most acceptance letters state that the sellers cannot receive sale proceeds or that the deal must close by a specific day and time.

Figure 9.1 is an actual student acceptance letter. The homeowners owed $67,000 and the property was worth $72,000. The offer was $25,000.

The bank will give you a deadline by which it must receive the short-sale payoff. Arrange the closing to take place prior to that stated date. Always use *your* title company or attorney whenever possible.

FIGURE 9.1   Bank Acceptance Letter

This is a student acceptance letter. The homeowners owed $67,000 and the property was worth $72,000. The offer was $25,000...

September 30th

Litton Loan Servicing

RE: Loan # 89543780

Dear Mr. Investor:

Litton Loan Servicing has agreed to participate in the assisted short sale of the above referenced property. The following terms must be satisfied prior to the closing of this transaction:

1.   The purchaser is agreeing to pay $29,000.

2.   The net proceeds to Litton Loan Servicing must not be less than $27,290 in the form of a cashier's check or certified funds payable to LLS.

3.   The closing proceeds must be in our office on or

       before October 30.

4.   LLS will provide a satisfaction of debt.

5.   **The current mortgagor is not to receive any proceeds from the sale of this property.**

6.   LLS is entitled to all reimbursements of escrow or other funds not reflected on the HUD closing statement.

7.   Closing agent must provide a copy of the HUD closing statement to LLS at least 24 hours prior to closing.

Closing agent MUST express deliver (by overnight carrier) proceeds check along with copy of final executed HUD settlement statement immediately following closing.

Upon receipt of funds and documentation previously specified, LLS agrees to release the mortgage pertaining to the above referenced property. Should you have any questions, call me at 555-5555.

Sincerely,

Jane Doe

Loss Mitigation Department

TIP: It's a bad idea to wait until your last day to close in case something happens and you need a few more days.

Should you need a few extra days, have the title company or attorney call the bank and ask for the extension. Typically, if the title company/attorney asks for it, it won't cost you anything. If you ask for it, you'll have to pay the daily per diem, which could run into the thousands of dollars.

TIP: When the bank agrees to accept your offer, ask what its per diem rate is just in case you can't close on time.

Be sure all the necessary people are present at the closing and that the money is there. Once the property is closed, you can rehab and retail it, keep it for long-term rental, or do what we do: wholesale it quickly.

FYI: We make most of our real estate money combining two techniques: We short-sale the deal and then wholesale it to a rehabber.

Please note that if you want to wholesale your short-sale property at closing, you must coordinate a double or simultaneous closing with your closing agent and buyer. We'll talk more about this soon.

In a nutshell, the rehabber comes to the closing with cash, and you buy the property from the homeowner and immediately sell it to the rehabber. The rehabber's funds pay for both transactions. When interviewing title companies or attorneys, ask them if they do double closings. If they say no, they are not investor friendly, so keep looking.

How Do I Buy More Time?

There are several reasons you'd need to buy time in a short-sale:

➤ The sheriff's sale is so close there is no time to negotiate a short-sale.

➤ You were unable to secure a buyer to wholesale the property to.

➤ You need more time to secure your financing.

Often homeowners will call you three days (or closer) to their sale date. Don't walk away! Call the bank and see if it will agree to postpone or cancel the foreclosure sale in order for short-sale negotiations to be completed.

TIP: When an extension is granted, you *must* get it in writing and fax it to the bank's attorney so that the sale will be canceled.

Banks often forget to notify the attorneys that they are postponing or canceling the sale to accommodate short-sale negotiations. The attorney shows up at the sale and the property is sold to the highest bidder. When this happens, you just lost your deal.

We fax the extension letter ourselves, because we never assume someone else has done their job. We have had several extensions granted only to find the property sold anyway. Someone in the chain did not fax an extension letter to the court or the attorney, and the property went to the highest bidder.

If you haven't found a rehabber or landlord yet, have the title company or attorney call and ask for an extension.

➤ Have your closing agent request the extension, stating title problems or trouble meeting requirements, which are typically the case. Ninety percent of the time, the closing agent can get an extension from the bank much more easily than you can. To avoid needing an extension, plan to close prior to the bank's deadline to allow a little leeway.

If you still need time to secure financing, again, have the title company make the call. If the closing agent cannot buy time, you'll have to pay the daily per diem. Don't forget to call the bank the day before the closing and short-sale the per diem.

You can usually get the bank to accept 50 percent or so of the per diem. "One more phone call" is your new motto in life!

There will be times when you will need a 20- or 30-day extension. The bank will not typically give a long extension without a charge, so know that figure going in.

➤ *Always* get the extension and the per diem charge in writing from the bank.

➤ Bottom line: Be sure you take control of every aspect of your deal. You notify the attorney or the bank of any change in the sale date.

Your paycheck depends on it!

This material works! I took the live three-day short-sale boot camp and went to work. I found a property within two weeks, did a short-sale for 36 percent of retail value, and closed it! I was happy when the loan company called to say it was a pleasure to deal with a professional!

Dominick "Bobby" Knight, Virginia

How Does the Homeowner Buy More Time?

It's surprising how many homeowners will call the day before the sheriff's sale asking for help. There is not much you can do with such short notice. The most successful strategy we have seen sellers use is bankruptcy. We are not advocates of bankruptcy; however, due to time constraints, it may be the homeowners' only option.

Have your homeowners speak to a bankruptcy attorney about filing a Chapter 13.

FYI: Filing a Chapter 13 bankruptcy enables the reorganization of debt.

Homeowners can go to the courthouse in person and file the bankruptcy papers themselves. Bankruptcy court may not be at the same courthouse where the foreclosure files are. Typically, bankruptcy court is in the federal courthouse and the foreclosures are handled in the county courthouse. In some of the smaller areas, both share a building.

Homeowners can get the do-it-yourself forms online, take them to the courthouse, and file the papers themselves. This will stop the sale and give the homeowners an opportunity to reorganize their debt and give you time to complete a short-sale.

When suggesting bankruptcy to a homeowner, you have to be very careful. There is a fine line between expressing an opinion and giving legal advice. This is the basic conversation we have with homeowners about bankruptcy:

We say, "Obviously, you realize that you would call an attorney to file bankruptcy for you. There is a free government web site at www.uscourts.gov that can explain your options to you. If you decide this is something you want to do, call me after the papers are filed and the sale is stopped and I'll see what I can do to help you."

It is important for you to understand that if you download the papers, drive the homeowners or their papers to the courthouse, pay the filing fees, or anything along those lines, you could be held accountable for practicing law. Although the homeowner loves you today, if this deal goes south, suddenly you will be the biggest jerk in the world tomorrow.

We have given this suggestion to many homeowners who have called late in the game.

We always call the bank first and ask for a postponement of the foreclosure sale. If the bank will not postpone the sale, bankruptcy is the only way to stall the foreclosure sale. When a homeowner files bankruptcy, a case number is assigned to the homeowner. The case number lets everyone involved know that the bankruptcy was actually filed. The bottom line is that without a case number, the sale will happen. If you live in a state with a short foreclosure period, like Texas or Georgia, you need to learn as much as possible about bankruptcy. With a short time-frame, you'll find it more difficult to do short-sales without basic bankruptcy knowledge.

Once the Chapter 13 papers are filed, the court will set a 341 hearing.

FYI: The 341 hearing in a Chapter 13 bankruptcy will be set in approximately 30 to 45 days and is for the benefit of the creditors.

The property can't be sold at the sheriff's sale until there has been a hearing. The purpose of the 341 hearing is to give the creditors a chance to present their cases and the homeowners a chance to show the bankruptcy judge that they have figured out a solution. Selling the property to you would be an acceptable solution for the judge.

It is hoped that this will be enough time for you to work out a short-sale and help your homeowners. If you have solved the problem in this time frame, the homeowners' bankruptcy attorney can drop the case and get them out of the bankruptcy.

The attorney will explain that if they miss the hearing they will be kicked out of bankruptcy and will not be able to file again for 180 days. If they drop the bankruptcy or ask for a dismissal, they can refile immediately if needed.

If you are still negotiating with the bank or trying to obtain financing, the homeowners' bankruptcy attorney can petition the court for an extension just before the 341 court date. Judges will typically grant at least one 341 extension, which gives you another 30 to 45 days to help your homeowners.

If you still haven't finished the deal, the homeowners' bankruptcy attorney can begin the bankruptcy process. At the hearing, the judge will put the homeowners on a repayment plan. As long as they make the scheduled payments, their property is safe from the sheriff's sale.

From the bank's point of view, the repayment plan is a forced *forbearance agreement*. When your short-sale is accepted, the bankruptcy trustee can take the sales contract and approval letter to the judge and have the property released from the bankruptcy, so that you can close.

➤ In a Chapter 13, if the homeowner does not keep up with the agreed-upon payments, the bankruptcy will be discharged and the foreclosure process will continue.

➤ The reality about filing a Chapter 13 first is that after several months the homeowners' bankruptcy attorney can roll it over to a Chapter 7 and extend the time.

FYI: A Chapter 7 bankruptcy absolves debt.

As with a Chapter 13, a Chapter 7 also postpones the foreclosure sale. When the homeowners get close to the end of the Chapter 7, the foreclosure process picks up where it left off. The banks are notified of the pending discharge. Since most banks can't keep up with their paperwork, more time will pass before the bank continues its foreclosure process. Again, this will give you a few more months to negotiate.

During this process, your homeowners' bankruptcy attorney can dismiss the bankruptcy at any time and save what is left of their credit.

Can you see why banks hate it when homeowners threaten bankruptcy? They know the homeowners can start with a Chapter 13, fall out of the 13, and then roll it to a Chapter 7, stalling the foreclosure sale for months and even years.

As we said earlier, we don't advocate bankruptcy. We don't want to make a bad situation worse. Sometimes bankruptcy is the *only* way to stop the foreclosure sale. The bottom line is to help the homeowners any way possible.

Remember, you are not an attorney (and neither are we), so be very cautious when talking to homeowners about bankruptcy. You don't want to get sued for practicing law without a license.

In most states, a bankruptcy can be filed one hour before the sale and stop it. Check with your federal courthouse or local bankruptcy attorney to see if this is true in your area. It's not a bad idea to take a bankruptcy attorney to lunch to familiarize yourself with the laws and how they affect the sheriff's sale in your state.

Bankruptcy court is federal, so the laws are the same nation-wide. What varies from state to state is how bankruptcy can be used to the homeowners' benefit in the foreclosure process.

At this point you are probably wondering how the new bankruptcy laws affect short-sales. The new bankruptcy laws really have no bearing on what we do. The new laws are designed to make it difficult for people with a lot of unsecured debt (like credit cards) to wipe away debt. Too many people were running up $200,000 in credit card debt, buying everything, even opening businesses, and then wiping it all away. The court system put a stop to it.

Look at what Jim and Gary have to say about buying time.

Dear Dwan and Sharon:

We wanted to thank you for changing our lives as investors. Learning how to negotiate short-sales opened an entire new avenue of income for us, not to mention how many more homeowners we can help.

We wanted to share a story that we probably will never forget. We did short-sales on 12 out of 16 houses that one seller owned! We found him by door knocking folks in foreclosure and met his tenants, who gave us his contact information.

The most difficult part of the deal was that each house had a different foreclosure sale date. Some of our negotiations required more time than the upcoming foreclosure sale date allowed. Sharon and Dwan taught us how to get extensions, so we got the extended time we needed. The owner had filed three bankruptcies, and usually lenders don't like to negotiate under a bankruptcy. With the help of Bill Twyford's negotiating in bankruptcy material, we were able to successfully persuade the lenders to continue the process anyway.

We used all the forms from the short-sale course, like the sample hardship letters, cover letter example to the lenders, income and expenses forms, and property repair questionnaires. We also followed the instructions exactly as taught in the course.

Doing all that allowed us to purchase 12 of the 16 properties. We used three exit strategies to maximize our profits. We wholesaled four right away to make some quick cash and earned $67,000. We sold one to a retail buyer immediately after renovating it and profited $11,000. Last, we purchased and kept seven *properties as rentals, taking $91,000 out in cash when we re-financed them after renovations were complete. We profited an additional $140,000 when we sold them two years later. We also earned $17,000 in positive rental cash flow.*

Our total profit on all 12 properties was $326,000! Overall, this deal was a win-win-win. The owner won by getting rid of 12 house headaches. He was extremely grateful to us for getting those burdens off his back. The lenders won because they unloaded 12 nonperforming, money-losing liabilities from their books. We won by earning $326,000!

We have since done hundreds of short-sale deals over the past five years and made millions *of dollars! Thank you, Sharon, Juan, Dwan, and Bill!*

Gary Prescott and Jim Izzolo

CHAPTER 10

Three Profit-Making Exit Strategies: Wholesaling, Rehabbing, and Renting

In this chapter, we discuss in more detail our three favorite ways to make money on our properties. It is important at this point to determine what your personal goals are:

➤ Do you want to specialize in wholesaling?
➤ Do you intend to rehab your own properties?
➤ Do you want to be a landlord?

We do all three. We started out as full-time rehabbers, but soon discovered wholesaling. Wholesaling is a much easier way to earn a living. We also keep rentals, and although we're not crazy about being landlords, we realize that having rental properties is a great way to build wealth and long-term paychecks. The good thing about being a landlord is that the money comes in even when you take the day off!

Pick your exit strategy and excel in that area. For example, the bulk of our investments involve wholesaling, but we also take on a couple of rehab projects along with five to 10 new rentals each year. If we look at a property and determine that it won't fit any of those areas we're interested in, we won't get involved. This doesn't mean that it won't be a good deal for someone else, though. Keep a network of investors to whom you can give your unwanted leads and make a finder's fee. We try to make money on every call we get, even when it is not a deal we want for ourselves.

The Wholesale Path

This is truly our favorite way to make money in real estate. The great thing about wholesaling is that you don't take ownership of the property. Rather, once you have the property under contract, you assign or sell the contract to another buyer who will then close on the property in your place. There is no risk involved, and you can do this with little or no money! Some people refer to this as "flipping." Regardless of the term you use, this is a way to make big money from a property you don't even own.

Let's look more closely at this process.

Step 1: Find a Distressed Property

We have already discussed easy and inexpensive ways to find distressed properties. If you are properly advertising, your phone will be ringing off the hook. Find a property with sufficient equity and get started. If there is no equity, you will begin the short-sale process.

Say you find a property that is worth $100,000 in market condition. You have negotiated the price down to $55,000 with the homeowner. Fill out a sales contract with the seller. In the "Buyer" or "Purchaser" section, follow your name with "and/or assigns." This will allow you to assign the contract to a rehabber. In order to make this contract binding, you have to leave a deposit with the homeowner at the time of signing the contract. We typically leave a $10 deposit.

You may ask, "Who would want just $10?" Everyone would. No one to this day has ever given us any grief for offering $10 as a deposit. It is best if you say it this way:

"We typically give $10 as a deposit, and will close in 45 days. That won't be a problem, will it?"

We have never had anyone not say okay to this. The only way they would reject the deposit is in how you presented it.

Step 2: Locate a Buyer/Rehabber

Start building your buyers list. This is a list of rehabbers to whom you can wholesale your properties. You obtain this list by running ads in the newspaper. Here are several samples of ads that you can run:

Handy investor special—great deal for rehabbers!
555-555-5555

Investor special—thousands below market! Won't last!
555-555-5555

I have a house in foreclosure. Please help! 555-555-5555

When investors or buyers call in, get all the pertinent information from them, such as:

➤ Name, phone number, fax, e-mail address, and postal mail address.

➤ Are you looking for a specific area?

➤ Can you close immediately with secured funds or lending?

➤ What is your price range?

➤ What level of rehab are you interested in—minor, remodeling, or major repairs such as foundation/fire damage?

➤ How many rehabs are you planning to do in a year?

➤ Are you interested in any rentals?

➤ What are your criteria for rentals?

➤ Can I call you with deals that I find? I'm sure we will be able to work together to find the right property for you.

Then, put all of that information into a database. Run your buyers list ad for two or three months. Even if you sell the property the next day, keep the ad running. When calls come in and the property is sold, tell callers that you are working on other deals and will call them once the deal is finalized. The buyers/rehabbers will always say okay. You will be surprised just how many names you will accumulate in a short amount of time. Keep these names handy, and when you run into another deal, e-mail or fax your list of buyers. The faster you find a buyer, the faster you get paid!

Step 3: Negotiate the Deal

Negotiate a deal with your rehabber and put it in writing! This is how a wholesale transaction might look:

- ➤ Let's say the property is worth $100,000 in market condition.
- ➤ Say the homeowners are distressed because they are behind in payments and/or facing foreclosure. They have to move quickly.
- ➤ Say the homeowners owe $50,000 on the property and they need $5,000 to move to pay for the deposit on their new place. (You know this because you asked them what they expected as a result of your help.)
- ➤ You offer the homeowners $55,000 and they accept.
- ➤ The house is worth $100,000 in good condition and you figure it will take approximately $15,000 in repairs to get it to market condition.
- ➤ You have a rehabber ready who will pay 65 percent of the retail value.
- ➤ You wholesale the property to the rehabber for $65,000 and make $10,000 for your assignment fee.
- ➤ The rehabber then will handle the repairs of the home and make the difference between the $65,000 purchase price and whatever the rehabber sells the home for.
- ➤ If the rehabber planned this well and keeps the repair costs moderate, there is a potential for the rehabber to make a profit of $15,000 to $20,000.

Not bad for everyone involved!

The contract you use with the rehabber is called an "Agreement for Assignment of Contract." It is a simple form that allows you to assign your contract without hassles. Your sales contract, through the Board of Realtors, may also be assignable—check your contract for the terminology used. If it does not specifically state that it is *not* assignable, then it automatically *is* assignable.

The key to putting together a successful wholesale deal is for the seller to have some moving money, for you to make an assignment fee, and for the bulk of the profit to go to the buyer/rehabber since he or she is the one taking the risk. It is better to make a small amount and turn many houses than it is to make a larger amount and move only a few homes.

Step 4: Close the Deal

Prepare for the closing using your investor-friendly title company. The beauty of a title company is that they do all the work for you. All you have to do is find the deal, wholesale it to a rehabber, and go to the closing! The title company does the rest. It is that simple!

We are sure that by now, you are asking yourself why a person with so much equity would walk away. Homeowners are in a different place mentally than we are. They have fallen behind on their mortgage payments; tried for months to make up the back payments, with no success; waited until they were *in* foreclosure to call a mortgage broker to refinance the property, which is too late; tried to sell using a real estate agent, but the house is in too poor condition to sell quickly; and then they see our ad.

At this point they just want out. Mentally, they have lost the personal attachment to the property and don't care anymore. This is why it is so important for you to be fair to homeowners. Once life gets back to normal and they have a chance to reflect, you want them to feel as though they got a good deal, too.

The Rehab Path

Rehabbing is an awesome and fun choice as well. The time to get started is immediately after the closing. Put a "For Sale by Owner" sign in the yard that day. When the calls start to come in, ask the prospective buyers if they prefer to see the property during the construction process or after completion of necessary repairs. Some buyers may want to pay less for the property but handle the repairs themselves. If you are lucky enough to have found a buyer right away, be sure that the buyer is going to pay cash or that the property will pass a lender's inspection as it is currently. Keep in mind that you will be able to ask a higher price after the repairs are completed.

We find that buyers are more apt to sign a contract after the home is in beautiful condition and staged. If this is your first rehab, bear in mind that you will probably make a few mistakes. We hope our tips will help you avoid making costly errors. The biggest mistake new rehabbers make is to overdo the remodeling of the home. The best piece of advice we can give you is to keep it simple. Remember, *you* are not the one who will be living there. Women tend to want to overdo the remodeling more than men. We also tend to overspend!

Here are some tips to help you with your first rehab project:

- *Locks.* Change the locks and put a lockbox on the door. The front panel of the lockbox has a combination that can be changed at any time. You can give contractors the code during their work, and then immediately change the code once they are finished.

- *Neighbors.* Introduce yourself to the neighbors in the area. They will be delighted to meet the person who will be fixing up the neighborhood eyesore, and may also know of a potential buyer. Exchange phone numbers with them and ask if they would be willing to keep an eye on the property for you.

- *Utilities.* Arrange for the utilities (gas, electricity, and water) to be turned on the day of the closing. Give the utility companies your mailing address. Don't have bills sent to the property address.

- *Yard maintenance.* Arrange for major maintenance such as lawn care or cleaning a pool. If you have the time, you can cut costs by doing this yourself.

Remodeling

Be sure you have permits if needed, and plan to start the project the day after closing (rather than on a specific date, in case there are any delays). Before you begin remodeling any property, take into consideration the neighborhood, your asking price, how much equity is in the property, and what your budget needs to stay at for this project.

Next, assign where your remodeling dollars will go. For example, if the home needs a roof, that is a major repair and should be done first. If the home has three bedrooms and only one bath, it may be in your interest to put in a second bath or completely remodel the single bathroom. Planning ahead will help keep you from going over budget. The more personal touches you put into your rehab, the more money that comes out of your pocket when the home is sold. *Keep your remodel simple, clean, and livable for anyone.*

Your home may be the closest thing to a new home most people will ever own. The newer the home looks, the faster it will sell. This means that you may need to *modernize* the home. Use current colors and accessories, and get rid of the old things that date the home, such as the dark 1970s cabinets, blue bathroom tile, or wood paneling in the basement! Put in something new and fresh, and it will make your home that much more marketable.

Curb Appeal

Curb appeal is very important when trying to sell your property. The exterior of the home needs to be attractive to prospective buyers so that they are enticed to enter the home. Paint the exterior of the home with neutral colors and complementary trim colors. Here are a few combinations that work well:

> White home with dark gray or black trim.
> Tan home with hunter green or maroon trim.
> Light gray home with white trim.
> Light yellow home with white or maroon trim.
> Sage green home with light gray trim.

Pay close attention to the region you are working in when choosing your color scheme. For example, in Florida you can get away with bright and vivid colors, whereas in Colorado or Arizona you would want to stick with earth tones. The best thing to do is visit the neighborhood and surrounding areas and see what other people have chosen for their homes. Also check the neighborhood covenants, as some areas have restrictions on color schemes. A rule of thumb is to paint the house a light color because it makes the home appear larger and cleaner. If you wish to enhance the charm of a historic house, you can do the opposite: paint the home a dark and warm color with a bright trim. You can also paint the doors or shutters a third complementary color to add character to the home.

Always place new street numbers on the home; they should be large and visible from the street. Change the outdoor lighting as well, or put a porch light in if there isn't one now. If an old mailbox exists, replace it—unless it is in good condition, in which case we recommend painting it the color of the trim on the home.

Interior Colors

Always use neutral colors for the interior of the home. This way, the home is not personalized to your taste, and anyone who walks in can see potential in the home. Again, the lighter the colors you choose, the larger the home will appear.

Do not use wallpaper—*ever*. Keep it simple and clean by painting the walls and ceilings, and replacing cabinets or painting the cabinet doors to brighten them up. You should always choose a satin finish for walls, and a semigloss finish for trim, bathrooms, and the kitchen. If there is dark paneling in the home, you don't have to remove it, but paint it a white or cream color to brighten the room.

When reviewing the ceilings, decide whether painting, a new popcorn finish, or texturing will offer the best results for the home and be most cost-effective. If popcorn exists on the ceilings now and does not need repair, just give it a fresh white coat of paint with a paint sprayer.

If walls are in disrepair, make sure they are patched and free of obvious rough spots. Another alternative is to give the walls a new knock-down texturing. It isn't difficult to do, and all the supplies you need can be purchased at a local home improvement store. You can paint directly over this texturing without having to put a prime coat on the walls.

Converting or Adding Rooms

If your home has a room that could be converted into a bedroom, add a closet and you will increase the value of the home. The building code requirements (in some states) for a legal bedroom are that the room has a door, heat, ventilation (window), and a closet. Check your state for the requirements before proceeding.

If the home has two bedrooms with two baths and a single-car garage, consider making the garage into a third bedroom. However, before you do that, research the area (comps) and find out which is selling better—homes with more bedrooms or homes with a garage.

You may also consider knocking a wall out to open up a room or make a larger living area. Again, this is something you can do yourself and relatively inexpensively.

Kitchen

The kitchen is an important selling point for any home, as it is a major living area for most people. If the kitchen is outdated, try painting the cabinets first. If you don't like the results, then you can reface the cabinets with a current-style door. If you have old appliances, change them! No one wants to have an avocado green stove anymore. However, this does not mean that you have to purchase new appliances. Some stores recondition appliances, and others offer great savings on scratched and dented items. You may even find a great deal in the newspaper from someone who is moving, remodeling, or going through a divorce. Another option is to resurface your appliances, meaning the company will refinish the enamel to match your color scheme. This can cost as little as $75 per appliance, versus purchasing a new appliance for $200 to $500.

Bathroom

The bathroom is another major selling point in a home. Keep the bathroom as clean and fresh as possible with bright but neutral colors. If your home is older, replace everything from the toilet to the tile to mirrors and towel holders. Paint the entire bathroom white or cream and use a semigloss finish. If you need to, resurface the tub; that will save you money rather than replacing it.

Flooring and Carpeting

It is worth the expense to replace linoleum or vinyl tile with ceramic tile, especially in the kitchen and bathroom(s). Also consider ceramic tile in a smaller living room or home office, as it will make the room appear larger than if you put in carpeting. If you do recarpet the home, use a medium-grade carpet with good padding. The better the pad, the more expensive the carpet will feel when prospective buyers view the home. Just make sure that the carpet you choose is Federal Housing Administration (FHA) approved in case your buyer gets FHA financing. Carpet displays will state on the back if they are FHA approved.

Climate Control

Air-conditioning and heating may be nonexistent in older homes, but they are necessary no matter where you live in the United States. Everyone wants to be warm in the winter and cool in the summer. Allow your budget to ensure that these items are in the home before you sell the property. There are many companies that rebuild air-conditioning units for a fraction of the cost of new ones and will guarantee the units.

Windows

Often the windows in your homes will be outdated (for example, older single-pane windows). The loss of air and heat results in higher utility bills. It also is easier for burglars to break in because of the poor construction. Unless other homes in the neighborhood are selling with this type of window, plan on changing them. It may be costly, but the alternative is to reduce your asking price. If your windows are an odd size, use smaller ones instead of custom-ordered sizes. It is easy for a handyman to reduce the opening to fit a new, smaller window.

Roof

Most roofs are either shingle or tile. Both can be pressure-cleaned by a professional; however, the results are better on tile. Tile roofs cost more to replace, but can be painted with a coat of specialty paint that seals the cracks. Tile roofs also can be spot repaired. Shingle roofs don't cost as much new or when replacing shingles, but they don't last as long as tile does. With age, shingles peel up and leak. Occasionally, if a shingle roof is peeling but not leaking, we replace the shingles. Buyers love to know they are getting a new roof. From their point of view, a new roof is costly. Make sure you get a warranty with a new roof that can be transferred to the new owners. This is a good selling point.

Cleaning

Once repairs are complete, bring in the cleaning crew. Our crew cleans the home from top to bottom, including the windows and screens, and gives the home a real sparkle. We feel that a spotless home makes the best first impression. Everyone loves a home that smells clean and has that new carpet and paint smell.

As-Is Basis

Once we have completed our remodeling and repairs, we sell our homes on an as-is basis. Buyers are still entitled to inspections, but it is your decision whether to repair or change any items. Keep in mind that your decision could make or break your deal.

Overall, the home needs to appeal to all five senses:

1. It must have *visual* appeal, starting with the exterior of the home.
2. It must *smell* nice from new paint and carpet.
3. The buyers must feel like they are at home and want this house so badly they can *taste* it.
4. They need to *hear* how wonderful the neighborhood is, how many new items are in the home, and how reasonable the price is.
5. They need to *touch* the materials to judge their quality.

It doesn't hurt to have a sense of *humor* when you are showing the house, either! The better the potential buyers feel about being in the house, the more likely it is they will want to purchase it.

If you want a tip on how to modernize the home without a huge expense, visit new communities and look at the model homes. You will find that many of them tile or vinyl tile the foyers, baths, and kitchens and put medium-grade carpeting elsewhere.

Homes always appear larger when they are empty. This also gives potential buyers a chance to visualize their belongings in the home. It is more difficult to sell an occupied home, especially if the occupants are messy, have animals, or smoke. We suggest you keep a light or two on inside the home as well as the outdoor lighting. This will enable prospective buyers to view the home at night.

Selling the Home

Congratulations! Your home is finished and ready to sell! Here are some sample ads to run once you are at this point:

> **Newly remodeled 3/2. New everything! Seller will pay closing costs. Below market! 555-555-5555**

> **Beautiful 3/1. Newly remodeled—like new! Must see to believe! Won't last! Sellers will help. 555-555-5555**

We say the sellers will help with closing costs in all of our ads, because this helps our properties move faster. Most buyers have a difficult time saving 5 to 10 percent to put down on the home. If you can help with any of that, your home will move faster. This is where your investor-friendly mortgage brokers come in, as they can assist you in finding the right buying program for each buyer.

There are many creative buying programs available where the seller is allowed to:

➤ Give gift money.

➤ Pay a portion of the closing costs.

➤ Hold back a small second mortgage.

➤ Give a 3 percent repair credit.

Take time to learn about these programs. Once you are ready to close, your title company will do the rest for you.

The Rental Path

You want to be a landlord. Wow, you are brave! Just kidding. We are also landlords and keep rentals as backup income for our business. If you don't wholesale or rehab for six months, guess how much income is coming in? Right—none. Therefore, having rentals is our way to long-term wealth.

Having a rental plan will help you make wise decisions for your long-term goals. One of the biggest mistakes we see new landlords make is buying more properties than they can afford. Here is an example:

Say you buy three rentals. The monthly mortgage payment is $500 on each of them, and you rent each out for $700. You are excited because you are bringing a positive income of $600 per month. Suddenly, though, they all become vacant at the same time; five months pass and they aren't rented again. What are you going to do? Can you afford to make the mortgage payments on all three properties for five months? If not, don't become a landlord until you have liquid cash.

We love to use the Section 8 program of the Department of Housing and Urban Development (HUD), which helps lower-income people with a place to live. Many landlords don't like government subsidized-housing programs because they don't like the tenants who rent through those programs. However, as you may have noticed, we like to create win-win situations for everyone, and if we can help a tenant on subsidized rent have a better place to live than a small, cramped apartment, we do so. We have had great luck with our tenants through this program, as well. The key to successful renting is to *screen* your tenants. You can use the best rental application in the world, but if your potential tenants live like pigs, your place will be trashed in no time. Therefore, one of us shows up at the prospective tenant's current residence unannounced. We tell the tenants that we are here for an inspection of their property. If they do not let us in, we won't rent to them. We want to actually see how they live. If they know you are coming, they will clean their home and have the kids on their best behavior. If you arrive unannounced, you get to see the truth about their lifestyle.

If the potential tenants try to make excuses for why you cannot enter their home, let them know that you understand they are packing (etc.), but that if they don't let you in now, their application will be discarded. Believe us, there is a big difference between "packing" and living like pigs. Look at the kitchen floors, the dishes in the sink, the bathtubs and toilets. The condition of these items will give you a good idea of how your rental will look when they vacate later on. We are not interested in replacing or remodeling each time a new tenant moves in or out, as it can take up all of our profit for the year to do so.

So why do it? The great thing about owning rentals is that the mortgage balance is paid down by someone else. You get to build wealth over a long period of time and you get to take the deductions and depreciation on your taxes, potentially reducing your taxable income substantially.

If real estate investing is your passion, you want to make sure you do not fall into the trap of spending so much time managing your rental properties that you have no time to go out and invest in more properties. We accumulate most of our rentals from homeowners in distress. We tell the owners that we will make the mortgage payments on time for the balance of the loan if they will keep their names on the mortgage. We take their deed "subject to" the existing mortgage.

When you purchase a home, there is a name on the mortgage and a name on the deed. The person whose name is on the deed is the actual owner of the home. Therefore, if distressed homeowners deed their home to you, you are the new owner of their home, as we explained earlier. You bring the back payments current and keep the property long-term. Be sure to make the payments on time, as you don't want to adversely affect the credit of the persons who deeded you their property. You are supposed to be helping them, not hurting them.

We love "subject to" rentals. When we come across a property that is in great shape and not far behind in payments, we keep it.

CHAPTER 11

Setting the Closing Date and Making Sure the Closing Goes Smoothly

The bank said yes, you have it in writing, the contracts are signed, you have turned all your paperwork over to the closing agent (the title company, attorney, or escrow company), and you are ready to close.

So, what happens next?

Actually, the closing agent takes it from here. The agent does the title search, and makes any last-minute calls to all the parties in order to complete the closing.

FYI: The closing agent can close in as short a time as three days, but prefers longer if possible.

Remember when you signed the sales contract with the homeowners? You gave yourself 30 to 45 days to close. You then completed your short-sale, assigned the deal to a rehabber or landlord, and gave the papers to the closing agent. The closing agent will set the closing based on the closest date or the final date the bank has granted.

How do you close with the rehabber or landlord in 7 to 10 days when your contract states you are closing with the homeowners in

30 to 45 days? You can't sell something you don't own. It's easy! Call the homeowners and tell them that you are ready to close early. Remember, they are in foreclosure and will be happy to close early. The sooner they close, the sooner they can start sleeping again. We have never had a homeowner who refused to close early.

When you filled out your contract with the homeowners, you used the words *"closing on or before"* such and such date. When we are ready to close, everyone has to cooperate. As we said, this has never been an issue.

Your homeowners are getting bombarded with collection calls, late notices in the mail, and people serving them papers at their home. This is a very stressful time. They are grateful to close early.

Once the closing date has been established, the closing agent will call all the parties. When everyone arrives, the homeowners are placed in a separate room from the rehabber. You will go back and forth between the rooms making sure everyone is happy, and that they are signing their papers. There is no need for the distressed homeowners to meet the rehabber. We think it makes for an awkward situation. The homeowners are embarrassed enough as it is.

If for any reason our rehabber were to be a no-show, we simply give the homeowners $100 and tell them that there is a problem and that we will reschedule the closing as soon as possible. We give them the cash for two reasons:

1. To say we're sorry for the time they wasted.
2. To make up for any lost wages they may have incurred by taking time off from work to attend the closing.

It rarely happens. A rehabber who is a no-show or cancels loses the deposit paid. Not many people are willing to walk away from a $3,000 deposit. As we said earlier, if your rehabber doesn't show, you still have plenty of time to find another buyer.

TIP: Always plan every deal as if it will fall apart, so that if it does, you are prepared. Careful planning helps most deals go smoothly.

A prepared investor will find a way to make every deal work instead of losing it because the buyer bailed out.

A Successful Closing

The day of the closing is here. You are super excited to get your first check. Whether you are using an assignment of contract or doing a double closing, the results are the same. You are leaving with a check!

Because you have done your job, this day is fun and easy. The closing agent has prepared the paperwork, your rehabber is coming with cash, the homeowners are getting out of foreclosure and can start life over, and you are getting money.

The closing itself is simple. Everyone signs papers, the closing agent gives everyone copies of those papers, money is exchanged, and everyone leaves happy. There is not much to a closing. The closing agent does the work at this point.

The closing agents have fees associated with the closing. These fees are negotiable, so don't be afraid to ask for lower fees. Remember, at some point, you may be their biggest client, so ask for the world and take what you can get. Always make certain that all parties involved are happy with the results. You want the rehabber to buy again, and you want the homeowners to walk away with a good feeling about real estate investors.

The closing agent will handle everything. All you have to do is sign papers.

Always have your driver's license with you. The closing agent will need a copy for the file. It is to prove that you are who you say you are.

In some states, if you are married and doing a double closing, you and your spouse both have to sign the closing papers. Because you are taking ownership to a piece of property and you are married, it is considered joint property. Your closing agent will let you know if this is an issue in your state.

The same goes for a corporation. If you form a corporation with a partner, check to see if both of you have to sign closing documents. Usually just one party can sign any necessary papers. Again, this is information the closing agent can give you.

That's it! The closing is the easy part. Like we said, the closing agent does all the work for you. All you have to do is pick up your check and do it again.

Along with a little sunshine, sometimes a little rain must fall. These are a few of the rainstorms you might encounter trying to get your deals closed.

What If My Homeowners Change Their Minds?

Once in a blue moon the homeowners will change their minds. Just know that it doesn't happen often. Unless the homeowners come into some money, there would be no reason for them not to close.

In the many years we have been investing, we have had only a handful of homeowners who wanted out of the deal. Since we have a rehabber lined up to close and a paycheck waiting in the wings, we do whatever we can to keep the deal together. In the special clauses section of the contract, it states that we must close with the homeowners before we can close with the rehabber. This protects us from a disgruntled rehabber in the unfortunate event that our deal falls apart.

Let's assume that the rehabber gave us a $3,000 deposit and we spent it. We do not want to return it if the homeowners bail out.

TIP: Having the special clause that calls for us to close with the home-owners first, and for the rehabber to allow us time to find another deal if this one does not pan out, keeps us from having to return a deposit.

We repeat: If you plan each deal as if it will fall apart, you'll find that most of them do not, but you'll be prepared in the event there is a problem.

In the unlikely event your homeowners want out of the deal, find out why:

➢ Did another investor offer them more money?

➢ Did they come into some cash and are now able to keep their home?

➢ Are they trying to refinance and keep the home?

The only way we will let the homeowners out of the contract is if they have figured out a way to keep their home. Ultimately, being a real estate investor is about creating win-win situations. Although we hate to lose a deal, we love to see homeowners keep their home and rebuild their lives.

If they want out for any other reason, we tell them no and remind them that we have the right to sue them for **nonperformance** if they do not close. Once homeowners sign a contract, they are legally bound by that agreement. We could sue them and win if we really wanted to. Would it be worth it to sue? Probably not. The threat of a suit is usually enough to keep your homeowners in the deal. Again, this rarely happens.

Nonperformance Sales contracts give the buyers the opportunity to sue the homeowners and force them to close if they refuse to follow through on the contract. Likewise, the buyers have a penalty if they do not close: They lose their deposit—another reason to leave only a $10 deposit.

Most new investors worry that their homeowners will be offered more money and cut them out of the deal. We have a great speech we give the homeowners to prevent that from happening.

TIP: Once the contract is signed and we are certain our homeowners are in the deal with us, tell them about unethical investors and how to avoid them.

We say, "Bob and Sally, there are many unethical investors out there. Luckily, you found me and I am not one of them. Let me share with you what unethical investors do. They knock on your door, just as I did. They go over the numbers with you, just as I did. Then they find out you are already under contract with me, and instead of walking away, they encourage you to get out of the contract with me and sell your house to them.

"They promise you more money. Bob and Sally, we have gone through the numbers and you do agree with me that this offer is more than fair, don't you? But let's just say you get out of the contract with me and agree to sell these unethical investors your house because of the promise of more money.

"The day of the closing arrives and you are expecting a huge check. At the closing table, they tell you the numbers didn't quite work out the way they expected and, unfortunately, there is no money for you at all. They tell you to sign the papers anyway or you will lose your house at the foreclosure sale. Because these investors have set your closing date so close to your foreclosure sale date, you will have only two options:

"You could sign the papers to save your credit from foreclosure but then have to walk away with no money, or you could leave the closing and still have no money and a foreclosure on your credit report.

"Now, Bob and Sally, you don't want that to happen, do you? Look at it this way: If someone will cut me out of a deal, why wouldn't they cut you out, too? Really, think about it—why would they follow through with you? There is no reason.

"I have set your closing date several weeks before the foreclosure sale date to give us a window in case we need a few more days. Unethical investors will cut me out of the deal, and then close with you the day before the sale. That way, you would have no other option but to sign the papers and walk away with no cash to start over if that is what the other investors say.

"I have seen this happen many times in the past. I realize when someone makes an offer of more cash and homeowners are in trouble, it sounds great. You have to trust me on this one: Anyone who will cut me out will cut you out as well. If anyone comes to you and makes you an offer that sounds like this, promise me you'll call me right away. Okay, great—let's get this deal done!"

Many homeowners have called us saying that they were approached by other investors in this exact way. We had them so worried about being taken advantage of that they actually slammed the door in the other investors' faces. Sadly, though, we have had a handful of homeowners bail out on us, only to hear from them a few weeks later, crying and saying that this exact scenario happened to them and they were taken advantage of. It's a sad day, but they were forewarned. Greed can be a killer.

The bottom line is:

➤ With an open, honest, well-established relationship with the homeowners, this will be a nonissue.

Again, if your homeowners want out because they have solved their foreclosure issue, let them out and find the rehabber another deal. This is another reason we want you to have five to 10 deals working at any given time. If your homeowners want out of the deal, you can supply your rehabber with another property and keep him happy.

The key to successful wholesaling is to build a replicable business. The happier you keep the rehabbers, the more business you will do. We'd love to see you wholesale 50 properties your first year!

What If My Buyers Change Their Minds?

In the unlikely event your rehabber bails out, you simply keep the deposit and move on. We have never met a rehabber who willingly walked away from a big deposit; however, it could happen. If you collect a $500 deposit from your rehabbers and they find a better deal, they may walk away from such a small deposit. When you take a $3,000 or more deposit, even if they find a better deal, they are unlikely to walk away from a deposit of that size.

The best way to ensure that you actually get the deposit in your hands is to have the rehabbers make the deposit check out to the closing agent and sign a paper stating that the deposit is nonrefundable and that they agree and allow the closing agent to release the deposit to you immediately. The closing agent will prepare this document. Even though the sales contract states that the deposit is nonrefundable, we still want the cash in our hands. If the check is left in the closing agent's escrow account and the rehabber puts a claim on it, the money might be tied up for a few months while everyone tries to decide what to do with the money. Although the money is clearly yours, closing agents do not like to get involved in disputes.

If you simply have the funds released at the beginning of the transaction, this is a nonissue. Rehabbers who do not allow their deposits to become nonrefundable are not solid buyers. There is no reason rehabbers should have a problem with this unless they are still shopping other deals. The simple fact that the contract calls for you to find them another deal if this one falls apart should be enough. Again, the only reason your end of the deal won't close is because of the homeowners. As we said earlier, most homeowners do not bail out on deals. They want to be out of foreclosure as soon as possible.

If your rehabbers do bail out on the deal without a great excuse, simply take them off your list and don't do any more business with them. We'll give you a great example:

Several years ago a man whom we had never met (but who knew of us) called an investor we knew and tried to buy a house from him. The man told my friend that he had done business with us and that we had made $80,000 on a deal that we had partnered with him. Our investor friend believed this man and put a deal together with him. The bottom line is that this man tried to rip off our friend for thousands of dollars. When our friend called us to discuss the situation, we assured him that we had never met the man or done a deal with him. Because we own and run a Real Estate Investors Association (REIA) group (www.flreia.com), the man had used our names. We told our friend that in the future when someone claims to know us, just pick up the phone and confirm it with us.

We stepped in and made a few calls, and the deal fell apart. Our friend did not lose any money and learned a good lesson. We asked every investor we knew about this man and found out that he was trying to put several deals together with other investors as well. The end result was: All the deals fell apart and this man was out of business. Had we investors not stuck together, no telling how many people might have lost money.

When someone treats you right, tell everyone; and when someone treats you poorly, tell everyone. The more we stick together, the better our industry is. You need to look at other investors as friendly competitors. We know all of the investors in our area. We often bid on the same properties, and one of them may end up with the deal. Although we don't like to lose out, we're happy for them. We know another deal is around the corner for us and we move on. Many times we have helped these investors wholesale a deal because we had a buyer for the property, but lost the bid.

When we are bidding against other investors, it is typically on bank-owned properties, which we will talk about later. When we are working directly with homeowners, there is little or no competition.

One of the reasons we suggest you attend REIA meetings is to meet other investors in your area. You might get 10 calls from distressed homeowners in one week and be able to wholesale only five of the properties.

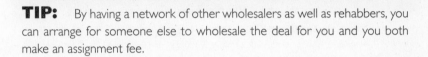

TIP: By having a network of other wholesalers as well as rehabbers, you can arrange for someone else to wholesale the deal for you and you both make an assignment fee.

We had one closing that had seven assignment fees on it—six other fees besides ours! We knew we should have charged more. It was a good day for all of us. We were all very surprised when it happened, because each of us did not realize the deal had been assigned so many times. We had a good laugh and went to lunch together. It was a fun afternoon and helped establish long-term business relationships.

Just remember to treat others as you want to be treated and that you reap what you sow.

Closing with the Assignment of Contract

Closing deals using the assignment of contract is our favorite way to close because we make the most money. (See Figure 11.1.) We make a net amount and do not have to pay any closing costs. When we do a double closing, which we will talk about next, we make the same fee except we have to pay closing costs. If our assignment fee is $20,000 using the assignment of contract, our check is $20,000. With a double closing, our net check might be $17,500—still good, but not the same.

There are pros and cons to using an assignment of contract.

➤ Our favorite pro: no closing costs.
➤ The downside: everyone sees what you are making, and banks rarely allow you to use one.

FIGURE 11.1   Sample Agreement for Assignment of Contract (Downloadable*)

THIS AGREEMENT FOR ASSIGNMENT OF CONTRACT (the "Agreement") is made and entered into as of the _____ day of _____, 20____, by and between **YOU, THE WHOLESALER**, (hereinafter referred to as "Assignor"), **YOUR REHABBER,** (hereinafter referred to as "Assignee"), with a mailing address of **REHABBER'S ADDRESS**.

WITNESSETH:

WHEREAS, Assignor, as "Buyer," entered into that certain Contract for Sale and Purchase (the "Contract") with **HOMEOWNER NAME**, as "Seller," a copy of which is attached hereto as Exhibit "A," for property with a physical address of: **PROPERTY BEING WHOLESALED** (the "Property"); and

WHEREAS, Assignee desires to purchase the Property for a purchase price of $ **THE PRICE YOU ARE ACTUALLY PAYING FOR THE PROPERTY. NOT THE PRICE YOU ARE WHOLESALING IT FOR** (the "Purchase Price") in accordance with the terms and conditions of the Contract; and

WHEREAS, Assignor desires to assign all of its rights, title, and interest under the Contract to Assignee as hereinafter set forth.

NOW, THEREFORE, in consideration of the sum of **TEN AND NO/100 DOLLARS ($10.00),** the mutual covenants contained herein and other good and valuable consideration, the receipt and sufficiency of which is hereby acknowledged, Assignor and Assignee hereby agree as follows:

A.   The above recitals are true and correct, including the recital of consideration.

B.   Upon the execution of this Agreement by Assignee and Assignor, Assignee shall give to **YOUR TITLE COMPANY** the sum of $**DEPOSIT FROM REHABBER**, which amount shall be considered an earnest money deposit (the "Deposit") hereunder toward the assignment fee, in the amount of $**WHAT REHABBER IS PAYING** – $**WHAT YOU ARE BUYING THE PROPERTY FOR** = the "Assignment Fee," to be paid by Assignee to Assignor as consideration for the assignment of the Contract set forth herein. At the closing of the Property pursuant to the Contract (the "Closing"), the original deposit paid by Assignor under the terms of the Contract shall be reimbursed to by Assignee to Assignor. If Assignee fails to close as provided herein and under the Contract, Assignor shall have the right, in its sole discretion, to terminate this Agreement and to retain the Deposit as agreed upon liquidated damages hereunder, whereupon the parties shall have no further obligations hereunder.

FIGURE 11.1 *(Continued)*

C. Upon payment by Assignee at Closing of the Purchase Price and the Assignment Fee, as well as the reimbursement of the original deposit to Assignor, Assignor shall deliver to Assignee or Assignee's agent an absolute assignment of contract (including all rights and benefits of the Buyer thereunder).

D. Notwithstanding anything to the contrary contained herein, the closing date under the Contract shall be held on or before **REHABBER'S CLOSING DATE. MAKE IT AS SOON AS POSSIBLE**, 20____.

E. Assignee hereby agrees, in writing, to assume and to be bound by all duties and obligations of the Buyer under the Contract, including but not limited to the payment of the Purchase Price and the payment of all closing costs to be borne by Buyer under the Contract.

F. Assignee hereby acknowledges and agrees **YOUR TITLE COMPANY** shall act as settlement/title agent for the transaction contemplated by the Contract, and Assignee hereby agrees to pay all sums, including but not limited to closing agent fees, title insurance premiums, title examination fees, title search fees and any other miscellaneous expenses incurred by the settlement/title agent for the purchase transaction contemplated by the Contract and this Agreement.

G. Assignee hereby acknowledges that Assignor is not in physical possession of the Property, has made no inspections thereof, and cannot and will not warrant the physical condition or any other matter regarding the Property, including but not limited to, the merchantability or marketability of the Property or its use for any particular purpose. In this regard, the assignment to be made by this Agreement is without recourse to Assignor, and, as between Assignor and Assignee, the sale of the Property is "As-Is, Where Is."

H. This Agreement shall be binding upon the heirs, successors and assigns of the parties hereto, and this Agreement shall be construed in accordance with the laws of the State of **YOUR STATE**. As to all matters hereunder, time is of the essence.

IN WITNESS WHEREOF, the parties have executed this Agreement as of the day and year first above written.

ASSIGNOR: _____   ASSIGNEE: _____

By: _____   By: _____

Name: Name:

Title: Title:

There will be times when your assignment fee is so large that you don't want everyone to see what you are making.

Let's talk about the assignment first. Typically, you'll make anywhere from $25,000 to $100,000 on each closing. In most areas, this is a reasonable assignment fee and should not upset anyone. When your fee is larger, you may want to consider a double closing. Your fee should be between 10 percent and 20 percent of the current retail value of the property. For example, if you are wholesaling a $200,000 property, your fee should be between $20,000 and $40,000. Not a bad day's work!

When using the assignment of contract, you will show up as an expense on the rehabbers' side of the **closing statement**. Closing statements have a Buyer side and a Seller side. In this instance, the homeowners are the sellers and your rehabbers are the buyers. Because the rehabbers are the actual buyers, you show up as a fee on their side.

Closing statement   Also called a settlement statement or HUD-1, this is the form signed by all parties showing the expenses related to the closing. A certified copy is always sent to the bank to confirm that the transaction has closed. This document is prepared by the closing agent.

Let's say you are buying the property for $100,000 and wholesaling it for $125,000. The rehabbers plan to fix up the property and sell it retail for $175,000. On the closing statement, the purchase price will be shown as $100,000, and you will show up as a $25,000 expense.

The purchase price remains the same as the purchase price on your contract with the homeowners. The assignment fee does not raise the actual purchase price; it is an expense. The rehabbers are paying you $25,000 for the right to purchase the property for $100,000.

If the rehabber is borrowing money to purchase the property, he shows the lender the assignment of contract and the sales contract. Rehabbers borrow money from hard-money lenders who are used to seeing assignment fees and have no problem with them. When the closing is complete and the deeds are filed at the courthouse, the sale price will show as $100,000.

How do you decide when to assign and when to double close? There are several determining factors. You would do a double closing if:

➤ The property is bank-owned.
➤ Your assignment fee is large.
➤ The bank accepted a short-sale.

It's very exciting for a wholesaler to find a property with a very low **loan to value (LTV)**. It means you can expect a larger assignment fee.

Loan to value (LTV)   What is owed against a property compared to its value. For example, if you owe $40,000 on a $100,000 property, you have a 40 percent loan to value. Likewise, if you owe $85,000 on a $100,000 property, you have an 85 percent loan to value.

At this point, many new investors wonder why homeowners with so much equity would walk away from it so easily.

When homeowners first get into trouble, they suffer from a major case of denial. They assume that they will figure it out and don't believe that the bank will actually take their house. They struggle with mortgage payments for several months and are finally served foreclosure papers.

At this point, many homeowners try to refinance the property or list it with a real estate agent. When the mortgage broker runs their credit report and sees that they are in foreclosure, the broker is unable to refinance the property. When the real estate agent sees that the property needs work, the agent is unable to sell it retail.

With time running out, the homeowners are looking for someone who can step in, right now, and solve their problem. This is why you will receive so many calls at the last minute. Homeowners often wait until it is almost too late. The great thing about wholesaling is that you can close deals in just days. It makes you very appealing to distressed homeowners.

Double or Simultaneous Closings

When you do a short-sale, you'll be doing a double or simultaneous closing. Instead of showing up on the closing statement as a fee, you'll actually buy and then sell the property. As we mentioned before, you would do a double closing if you are making a huge assignment fee, you are buying a property from a bank, or you got your short-sale accepted.

When the homeowners lose their property at the sheriff's sale, it becomes bank-owned. Once the bank takes the property, it will list it with a Realtor and sell it retail. We make low offers on bank-owned properties as well as dealing directly with homeowners. We'll talk more about bank-owned properties soon.

This is where new investors get confused. They think that since they are buying and selling the property, they need money. Not true. As we have said all along, you can do this business with just $10.

Let's say you are buying a property for $50,000 and selling it to your rehabber for $65,000 and you have to do a double closing. The day of the closing comes and the distressed homeowners and the rehabber show up. The closing agent places them in separate rooms just like a regular closing.

The rehabbers bring a check for $65,000 and give it to the closing agent. The representative for the closing agent takes the $65,000 check, puts it in the escrow account, and then disburses the funds properly.

The only difference in this closing is that you are in the chain of title. The homeowners are selling their house to you, and you are then selling it to the rehabber. You sign the closing statement as the buyer for $50,000, then turn around and sell it to the rehabber for $65,000. You make $15,000 minus closing costs. Your net check might be $13,500 instead of $15,000.

We want you to interview title companies, attorneys, and escrow agents regarding double closings. You must find a closing agent who will do double closings that are cost-effective for you as well as structure the deal so that using your buyer's money to fund both closings will be perfectly legal. Since the rehabber is the ultimate buyer, we see no need to pay extra closing costs.

The closing agent will charge for document preparation, deed prep, title searches, and so on. The agent charges each party a specific set of closing costs. There are costs associated with buying as well as selling. Since you are both buying and selling in this transaction and the rehabber is the ultimate buyer, the closing agent does not need to charge two sets of everything.

You must find out which fees are mandatory and which fees are negotiable.

For example, we buy properties in Florida and Colorado. In Florida, we have to pay a fee to transfer the deed; in Colorado we do not. This fee cannot be transferred to another. The person buying must pay it. In Florida, we pay $7 per $1,000 to transfer the deed. This means that if we buy a property for $100,000, we pay $700 to the county. If we were doing a double closing, we'd have minimum closing costs of $700.

Whenever a deed is transferred, a title search is done. As we mentioned earlier, there is a cost for this. Many investors don't think it is worth it to pay for title insurance in a double closing because you own the property for only a moment in time. Others are cautious and pay for it although it is unlikely it will ever be needed. Based on what you know of us, which way do you think we play the game?

Like we always say, if you handle every deal as if it will fall apart or have a problem, it never will. *We always get title insurance.*

Title insurance protects you financially should the title turn out not to be clear and free of liens and lawsuits. We have been in this business a long time and have seen many items missed on title searches. Should something come up later and you didn't purchase title insurance, you could be liable down the road.

In the worst-case scenario, you'd have to give back your profit. What if your profit was $50,000? If it were us, the money would be spent and we wouldn't have it to give back. We'd rather spend a few hundred dollars today knowing our money is safe and spendable tomorrow.

Don't forget—in a double closing there are two sales contracts.

One is between the distressed homeowners and you. The other is between you and the rehabber. With each contract you will use the special clauses that apply to that contract.

The closing will happen the usual way except you will sign two sets of papers: one as a buyer and one as a seller.

That's it! It's that simple.

Are Double Closings Illegal?

We speak to real estate investors across the United States every week. It stuns us how many investors think or have heard that double closings are illegal. If they were illegal, why would closing agencies be doing them? They absolutely are *not illegal* as long as you have proper disclosure.

When you wholesale a property, who is the actual buyer? Right, the rehabber. Whether you double close or use the assignment of contract, the rehabber is still the ultimate buyer. If the rehabber is borrowing money for this transaction, the lender needs full disclosure. The closing agent needs to tell the lender that it is funding two transactions:

1. The purchase between the homeowners and you.
2. The sale between you and the rehabber.

The closing agent will call the lender and disclose that this is a double closing. What can make a double closing illegal is if the lender is not told that it is funding two transactions. Many lenders have guidelines that do not allow funding for two transactions.

For example, if you were to call a conventional bank like Washington Mutual and state that you want to do a double closing, WaMu would not lend the money.

These types of banks do not allow funding for two transactions. They don't understand how you can buy a property for $50,000 and sell it for $65,000 10 minutes later. They are concerned about fraud and, therefore, won't fund two transactions.

Rehabbers borrow money from hard-money lenders. Hard-money lenders are in the business of lending to rehabbers and completely understand double closings and are happy to lend on them. They understand that rehabbers often purchase from wholesalers and that the wholesalers are making a fee for their service.

Another benefit of using investor-friendly closing agents is that they fully understand double closings and how to make them completely legal. We love the fact that the closing agent handles everything for us. However, it is important for you to be an educated consumer. Disclosure is only as good as the person doing the disclosing.

Make certain the closing agent has done its job properly. Ask if all disclosures have been made and then double-check with the rehabber's lender at the closing. Typically, the lender will attend the closing. We like to cover ourselves by making sure everyone knows what is going on. We don't want a legal issue tomorrow because disclosures were not done today.

Once you have established a good relationship with your title company, attorney, or escrow agent, you won't have to watch them as closely. We have had very good luck with the title companies we have used over the years. We used to refer other investors to the title companies that we really liked. The next thing we knew, they were too busy for our closings. Not that we are spoiled, but if we want to close in one day and close at 7:00 P.M., we want to be catered to. We are huge clients, bring a lot of business to the company, and are very busy ourselves. We need a company that will work around us, not expect us to work around them.

We have a great place now. The company sends someone to our office to do the closings. It's really great when you don't have to leave the office to collect your check. As you become a larger client, you'll find that closing agents will cater to you, as well.

CHAPTER 12

First-Year Expectations

Elliott has become one of our best students. He came to us while he was in a bad situation himself. Now he has made well over $1 million cash! What an accomplishment. Can you do as well as Elliott? You bet you can. In fact, we are counting on it.

Good Day, Dwan and Sharon:

It gives me great pleasure to share with the readers how your program has changed my life and has been very instrumental in allowing me to give back and help others change their lives, too. I have been a student of yours since the fall of 2004. And after studying, not just reading, the concepts/rules/procedures of the short-sale game, I was able to experience success before the end of the year to the tune of about $37,000 on three deals.

As 2005 began, which I call my second year in the business (first full year), I began to aggressively advertise via bandit signs, local print ads, car signs, apparel advertising, and word of mouth. One of my favorite deals that I got was a referral of a retired mother and her recently unemployed daughter, who were behind on mortgage payments and faced with the reality of losing their home when they were told to call me.

The daughter was in the mortgage business, doing most of her customers' loans out of state. Somehow her business began *to dry up and her attempts to revive it were not successful. We spoke about what her options were, and she decided to see if she could get something worked out on her own. She found out that she couldn't work out anything beneficial with her bank because it did not do short-sales. Instead, the bank was going to sell the note to an investor group that would do short-sales. When it did, she called and negotiated a short-sale with the new lender. She owed over $545,000, which included eight-plus months of back payments, late fees, and whatever else the lender could add on to make their situation seem hopeless. The principal balance was about $475,000 on her waterfront property.*

She called me, very excited that the new lender was willing to do a short-sale and that she had been able to get them to accept $515,000. I could buy it at that price or maybe slightly less. I informed her that I was glad that she had been able to get her new lender to agree to a short-sale; however, our company policy is to buy property at a price that we believe is a good deal. I told her that I would be willing to pursue the short-sale myself in order to reduce the payoff to a more favorable price for my clientele base. I then e-mailed the "Authorization to Release Information" form, which I had gotten out of your course, along with my contract to purchase.

Upon getting these items signed and returned to me, I contacted the new lender. To my surprise, I was able to talk directly to the managing partner of the company. As our conversation progressed, I could see the questions about value being brought to the forefront. I began to present my case just like the course states. (The key for me or any other student is to know the facts and have the rules embedded in you so when a similar situation arises, you can adapt the concepts to that situation.) Here's what I mean: The managing partner said that the lender was looking for about $500,000 for the house on the short-sale. I knew they had just bought this note along with several million dollars more of defaulted notes for about 30 cents on the dollar; this implied that *their exposure to the bad debt was minimal at most. I pointed out to him why this amount was unrealistic: The builder who built this home (along with most of the other homes around the lake) had gone bankrupt, and the land had been bought by another builder, who was continuing to build homes in the subdivision that were being sold at much lower prices. I referred to the comps I had sent him. I asked the managing partner if the lender had done a BPO [broker price opinion] on the property before buying it. He confirmed they had, and the value had come back at $300,000. Now mind you, he was asking $500,000 and he knew that the property was not valued at that amount.*

I told the managing partner that I did not want to make an offer on a property that could not get through underwriting. I told him that I would only be able to offer $275,000. The managing partner said that he would get back to me via e-mail with the BPO that they had and also let me know about the $275,000 soon. He contacted me a few hours later stating that the BPO was at a different location and it would take a couple of days to get it to me. In the meantime, he wanted to know how soon could we close if they accepted the $275,000. My response was 30 days, as the course teaches. I received an e-mail from the managing partner that said, "Let's do it."

Now, in these short-sale situations, the course states in so many words to expect the unexpected. Great advice! I had not secured a buyer yet, but I had several prospects in mind. I knew that within the prior 12 months a lakefront property in the subdivision had sold for $455,000. I accepted a contract from one of my investors for $325,000 with a $3,000 nonrefundable deposit (as the course suggests). Well, as life would have it, the buyer's credit score dipped below the 700 mark and his 100 percent loan was now 95 percent, putting the deal in jeopardy. I asked him if I could do anything to help on my end, because we were running out of time to close the deal. He needed more time to correct the situation or find a new lender. So, I put on my thinking cap and *had my Realtor team member (I'd learned about building your team in the course) pull the past six months' worth of comps, in which I discovered that the highest sale had dropped to $259,000. I then contacted the managing partner and told him that because of the change in comps, the underwriter needed a review appraisal of the property to ensure the value, which takes 7 to 10 business days to get back. He agreed.*

We got the buyer approved; however, I decided to do an altered version of the "one more phone call" that you teach. I sent the managing partner "one more e-mail" stating that the highest sale in the subdivision had dropped to $259,000. The managing partner replied that the lender could accept that price. The "one more e-mail" put another $10,000 or more in my pocket.

To wrap it up, I made $63,000 in about 75 days, with maybe 12 total hours of time spent. I also allowed the homeowners to stay in the property for four months at no cost so they could save some money.

This is only one of about 25 deals that I have closed in the past 27 months. I wish everyone reading this book the best of luck. If you put forth the effort, you can make this happen for you also.

Respectfully,

Elliott Anderson

How You Can Become Rich without Going to College

You don't have to go to college or have a degree to be a real estate investor! In fact, you don't need any real estate experience or even a real estate license! What you do have to do is read this book, learn these proven steps, and follow them.

You must also be *willing to work*. The investor fairy isn't going to drop deals in your lap. You have to run ads, read ads, knock on doors, work with homeowners, and put your deals together. The beauty about investing is that you don't have to work that hard at it.

It can seem overwhelming at first. Start with blue-collar, middle-of-the-road neighborhoods, as these properties are the easiest to sell.

They will vary by price depending on the area. Blue-collar neighborhoods are typically two-income households, filled with working-class folks. This does not mean you can't work other types of neighborhoods, but for the sake of having an opportunity to get started, begin with the properties that sell the best.

What We Did to Get Here

We both started from very difficult situations—one a single mom and one a young widow. Today, we both have assets that easily put us in the multimillion-dollar category. How did we do it?

> We worked *hard*.
> We were committed to our business.
> We set our goals and reviewed them each day.
> We kept track of our goals, checking off the ones we accomplished and added new ones for our future.
> We didn't let anyone talk us out of it.
> We refused to quit, even when it was tough. When we would run into an obstacle, we would figure a way around it instead of letting it stop us from accomplishing our goals.

A major part of our success is seeing things from the other person's point of view. We look at the mind-set of the homeowners, bankers, real estate agents, mortgage brokers—everyone. We try to understand what motivates them to work with us. When we know what their motivation is, we can work better and smarter to help them achieve what they want, while at the same time we achieve what we want. This creates the win-win situation that you should strive for through each of your deals.

Our typical week would consist of us meeting every Monday morning to review our goals and line up our week. Then we would spend a few hours knocking on doors of homeowners in distress. We would mail postcards to everyone who had a newly filed lawsuit such as bankruptcy, divorce, or probate, contacting them *before* they were in foreclosure. We would make phone calls to homeowners in distress, run newspaper ads, take incoming calls, and attend many networking and charity events where we met people to whom homeowners would turn for help.

Mortgage brokers became a good source of leads for us, because if there isn't enough equity in the home, they are typically not able to help the homeowner out with refinancing. Therefore, they would refer those people to us! We also networked with divorce attorneys, bankruptcy attorneys, foreclosure attorneys, and probate attorneys, as homeowners often use these services when in trouble.

We would also do all our paperwork, maintain our rentals, and send workers out to our rehabs in addition to taking calls from sellers and buyers. It was an extremely busy schedule, but completely worth our time!

Within a couple of years, we were able to move our offices out of our homes and into an actual office. It had become apparent that this transition needed to be done so that we could have an office presence. However, we do not recommend that a new investor go out and look for an office right away. Once you are on your feet making deals, then you can determine when it is right for you to move your business into an office.

We have treated this business as a business, working regular hours each day. If you want to become super-successful, then you have to put in the hours in a disciplined fashion. Being self-employed has its perks, though. You will be able to still enjoy eating out, shopping, and other fun things once you have deals coming in.

The income potential is limitless; the determining factor is how badly you want it. What are you willing to do to get it? The fact that you are reading this book is a first step. The next steps are to attend one of our nationwide boot camps, sign up for our newsletter (www.theieu.com), read our magazine (www.reipmag.com), and really jump-start your career. In addition, you should be attending every seminar that comes your way, and you should join your local real estate investment group (see www.flreia.com) and start *networking*. Since the average American makes $33,000 per year, $100,000 would be a great place to start, right? Increase your goals as well as your income each year in this business. Don't doubt your potential to earn $1 million in a year!

We specialize in training and coaching new and seasoned investors. We fully remember being new investors and therefore have written this book to help you learn this business, saving you time and (we hope) helping you avoid mistakes along the way. This business is so very exciting, and we are looking forward to your upcoming success!

What You Can Expect in Your First Year

We began this business through rehabbing. After a couple of years, we knew there had to be a better way than doing all the work ourselves! That's when we discovered wholesaling and it became our niche. The best part about wholesaling is that we never own the properties, and therefore have little or no money invested in them. Our first big check from a wholesale deal was $54,000. We couldn't believe it, and this with only a $600 deposit! We were hooked!

Believe us, you will get hooked, too. It will be so exciting for you that you will want to quit your regular job. Realistically, you could put a deal together and close it 30 days from today for $10,000 or more. For many, that is more than you would make in three months' time! Look at it this way: If you need $30,000 cash in order to quit your job (annual salary), try to wholesale four properties in the next two months. That should cover your expectations and maybe even more. The key is to keep the cash so that you have a buffer to become a full-time investor. The fact that you are reading this book puts you years ahead of where we started! We truly learned by the seat of our pants and made many, many mistakes along the way.

You will find that most investors are men. This is not a negative thing, but men and women approach this business completely differently. Men will go into the deal, offer the deposit, get the deed, and move on as quickly as possible—straight to the bottom line. Women tend to be nurturing, sympathize with the situation, and want to help people out. That is what has made us so successful in this business: doing what we feel is best for the homeowner even if it means we don't get the deal. So what is the point here? Try to get in touch with your feminine side (including you guys!), and have empathy for the people you will be working with. Although both sexes want to get to the bottom line as quickly as possible, sometimes the homeowners need someone to listen to them. Bite the bullet, and do what it takes to be patient with them.

Thinking Like a Millionaire

Are you beginning to see the benefits of being a real estate investor? Folks, if you do things right and have the right goals, the money will come to you. As you begin to make money in this business, here are some tips for you:

- ➤ Lead a good life—what goes around comes around.
- ➤ Keep a low profile (most millionaires are not blatantly obvious).
- ➤ Put money away to protect yourself and your future.
- ➤ Maintain balance in your life.
- ➤ Buy something you have always wanted ... because you *can* now.
- ➤ Be spontaneous!
- ➤ Take someone you love on a trip somewhere you never thought possible before.

The great thing about investing in real estate is that it doesn't have to be your passion. You can make full-time money in just a few hours per week. This can give you the time and the money to pursue your other interests and passions. Say you have always wanted to climb Mount Everest. Complete several real estate transactions and take the next year off to pursue this dream! Nothing is stopping you from achieving your goals now.

Then there are those of us who really find real estate investing our passion—there is nothing more exciting than the thrill of the deal! Knowing that you made a difference in someone else's life is exciting, too. We can't imagine ever doing anything else!

So, can you do it? We say yes. Your first step is to reread this book and make sure you understand what to do; then *do it*.

Make sure that each day you go to work you love what you do. You are giving up one day of your life for it, and you can never get this day back. Was work today worth giving up a day of your life? If not, make a change; we'll help you.

We love to help homeowners, and we love to help new students, like you, become successful. We are happy to give up a day for what we do, because we make a difference in someone's life every day; and you can do that, too.

May God bless and reward your business.

Acceptance letters, 83, 159–160

Accomplishments, 9–10

Advertising, 13–14, 43–47, 49–50, 171, 180

Agreement for Assignment of Contract, 172, 192–193

Air-conditioning, 178

Appearance, personal, 12, 55–56

Appraisals, bank, 105

As-is basis, 179–180

Asset managers, 119–120

Assignments of contract/assignment fees, 172–173, 191–196

Attorneys, 14–15, 65, 162, 163–166. *See also* Closing agents

Authorization to Release Information, 73, 75, 79, 90, 113–114

Bail bondsmen, 46

Balance in lifestyle, 8–9, 208

Bank accounts, 15–16

Bank-owned properties, 22, 39–43, 64–65

Bankruptcy, 65, 91, 139, 144, 163–167

Bankruptcy attorneys, 65, 163–166

Banks. *See also* Lien holders

acceptance from, 19, 21–23, 83, 159–160

appraisals for, 105

asset managers in, 119–120

closing costs and, 106

communication with, 113–115

debt *vs.* ownership and, 146–149

decisions from, 127–129

deeds in lieu of foreclosure by, 64–65

deficiency judgments by, 100–101

double closings and, 198–199

extension letters from, 162

forbearance agreements by, 61–62, 165

foreclosure process and, 149–150

hardship packages to, 123–124

listing agreements for, 124–125

loan modification by, 60–61

loss mitigation representatives in, 66, 90, 99, 114, 116–119, 121–122

negotiations with, 23–32, 66–67

offer presentation to, 115–119

portfolio representatives in, 120–121

proof of funds letters for, 126–127

relationships with, 20, 117–119, 121

Release Authorization to, 73, 75, 79, 90, 113–114

seller bankruptcy and, 163–166

shareholders and, 122–123

short-sale packages to (*see* Short-sale packages)

Bathrooms, 177

Bedrooms, 176–177

Bills of sale, 34–35

Budgeting, 13–14, 81, 174–175

Building code requirements, 176

Business. *See* Investors; Real estate investing

Business entities, 14–16, 84, 185

Buyers, 4, 67–68, 171–172, 179, 198–199

Buying programs, 180

Carpeting, 177–178

Case study, 2–6. *See also* Testimonials

Cash offers, 40–41, 126

Cash reserves, 22, 32

Cellular telephones, 13
Certificates of discharge, 87
Certificates of title, 104. *See also*
    Deed(s)
Certified final judgments, 153
Chapter 7 bankruptcy, 166
Chapter 13 bankruptcy, 65, 163–166
Cleaning, 179
Climate control, 178
Closing agents, 159, 161–163, 173,
    183–186, 189, 197–200
Closing costs, 105–107, 180, 191, 194,
    197
Closings:
    assignments of contract and,
        191–196
    bank deadlines and, 159, 161–163
    double, 161, 191, 195, 196–200
    per diem rates and, 86, 161–163
    prompt, 40–43
    rehabber withdrawal from, 189–191
    seller occupancy and, 36–38
    seller withdrawals from, 186–189
    setting date for, 183–184
    successful, 185–186
    wholesale transactions and, 173
Closing statements, 31, 105, 194
Clothing, 12, 14, 55–56
Colors, 175–176
Commissions, 124–125
Communication, 113–115. *See also*
    Listening skills; Relationships;
    Telephones
Comparable properties, 3–4, 40, 77,
    103–105
Contractor estimates, 107
Contracts, sales, 76, 79–80, 82, 84–86,
    91–97, 170, 198
Corporations, 14, 185
Costs:
    budgeting, 13–14, 81, 174–175
    closing, 105–107, 180, 191, 194, 197
    of closing agent fees, 185
    of repairs, 107–108, 174–175
Counteroffers, 129
Cover letters, 42, 99–102, 139–142
Credit reports, 5, 22, 63–64, 65
Curb appeal, 175–176

Deals, 6–7, 39–50
Debt *vs.* ownership, 146–149, 182
Deed(s):
    in lieu of foreclosure, 64–65
    ownership and, 104, 146–147, 182,
        197–198
Deed of trust state foreclosures,
    151–152
Deficiency judgments, 100–101
Department of Housing and Urban
    Development (HUD), 155, 181
Department of Veterans Affairs (VA)
    loans, 125, 155
Deposits, 41–42, 170, 184, 186, 189–190
Disclosure, 198–199
Double closings, 161, 191, 195,
    196–200

E-mail, 115
Equities of life, 7–8
Equity, 20
Equity/home improvement loans, 156
Escrow companies. *See* Closing agents
Ethics, 187–188
Exit strategies:
    rehabbing property as, 173–180
    rentals as, 180–182
    selection of, 169–170
    wholesaling as, 170–173
Expenses, managing, 13–14, 174–175.
    See also Costs
Extension letters, 162

Family, 10–12, 36
Fax, 13–14, 115
Federal Housing Administration (FHA)
    loans, 125, 155, 178
Financing, 126–127, 197. *See also*
    Banks; Liens; Loans; Mortgages
Finder's fees, 170
Flipping. *See* Wholesaling properties
Flooring, 177–178
Forbearance agreements, 61–62, 165
Foreclosable liens, 154
Foreclosure laws, 145
Foreclosures:
    bankruptcy and, 163–166
    on credit reports, 5

debt *vs.* ownership and, 146–149
in deed of trust states, 151–152
loopholes in process, 58–65
in mortgage states, 149–152
postponement of sales, 122, 162
Friends, 10–12, 117
Full-time employment, 10

Garages, 176–177
Gender, impact of, 57–58, 207
Goals, 7–10, 205, 208
Government subsidized-housing
programs, 181

Hard-money lenders, 126, 155, 194,
199
Hardship budgets, 81
Hardship letters, 80, 88–91, 98, 141–143
Hardship packages, 123–124
Heating, 178
Home improvement/equity loans, 156
Home offices, 13–14
Homeowners. *See* Sellers
Homeowners association liens, 154
Housing market, 3, 40, 78, 82, 103–105,
145
HUD (Department of Housing and
Urban Development), 155, 181
HUD-1 form, 31, 105, 194

Inferior lien holders, 131–132, 136–144,
147–149
Inspection periods, 40–41
Investors. *See also* Real estate investing
accomplishments of, 9–10
availability of, 13, 43–44
balance in lifestyle of, 8–9, 208
expectations of, 201–208
financing of, 197
as landlords, 180–182
motivation of, 6–7
networking between, 39, 44–45, 67,
145, 190–191
personal appearance of, 12, 55–56
as rehabbers, 173–180
self-promotion of, 13–14, 44–46,
49–50
as sellers, 180

strategies for locating potential
properties, 39–50
unethical, 187–188

Joint properties, 146–147, 185
Jones, Daniela, 3–5
Judgments, 100–101, 150, 153
Judicial foreclosures, 149–152
Junior lien holders, 131–132, 136–144,
147–149

Kitchens, 177

Landlords, 23–24, 180–182
Land trusts, 182
Legal issues. *See also* Attorneys
bankruptcy as, 164–167
business structure and, 14–15
with double closings, 198–199
foreclosures and, 145, 149–152
ownership and, 146–149
seller nonperformance as, 187
"subject to" agreements and, 64
Letter of Intent, 42
Lien holders. *See also* Banks
junior, 131–132, 136–144, 147–149
priority of, 148–149
Release Authorization to, 73, 75, 79,
90, 113–114
Liens, 152–154. *See also* Loans;
Mortgages
Lifestyle, balance in, 8–9, 208
Lis pendens, 153–154
Listening skills, 52–53, 55, 57, 207
Listing agreements, 124–125
Loans, 60–61, 83, 120, 125, 139,
155–157, 178. *See also* Liens;
Mortgages
Loan to value (LTV), 131, 155,
195–196
Locks, 174
Loopholes in foreclosure process,
58–65
Loss mitigation representatives, 66, 90,
99, 114, 116–119, 121–122

Magnetic vehicle signs, 45–46
Mailings, 45

Market, housing. *See* Housing market
Mechanic's liens, 154
Mortgage brokers, 180
Mortgages, 131–132, 136–144, 146–149,
    154–157, 182
Mortgage state foreclosures, 149–152
Motivation:
    of investors, 6–7
    of sellers, 51–54, 173, 196
Move-out dates, 36–38
Moving expenses, 35–36
Municipal code violations, 154

Negativity, 10–12
Negotiations:
    with banks, 23–32, 66–67
    with junior lien holders, 136–144
    with rehabbers, 172
    with sellers, 33–38, 54–57
Neighbors, 174
Net sheets, 105–107
Networking, 44–45, 67, 170, 190–191,
    205–206
Neurolinguistic programming, 55
Newspaper advertisements, 43–44, 171,
    180
Nonperformance, 187

Occupancy by sellers, 36–38
Offers:
    calculation of, 23–25, 32, 172–173
    cash, 40–41, 126
    justification of, 3–4, 40–42, 69,
        77–78, 80–82, 88–91, 98–111, 114
    presentation to bank, 115–119
Office, establishing, 13–14
Option adjustable-rate mortgages,
    156–157
Ownership *vs.* debt, 146–149, 182

Paint, 175–176
Partnerships, 14–15, 185
Pawnshops, 46–47
Payment plans, 61–62, 165
Payoff acceptance, 83
Payoff notes, 27
Per diem rates, 86, 161–163

Personal appearance, 12, 55–56
Photographs, 98–99, 100, 101
Portfolio representatives, 120–121
Positions, 147–148
Postcards, 45
Preapproval letters, 126–127
Private loans, 155. *See also*
    Hard-money lenders
Proof of funds letters, 126–127
Properties:
    bank-owned, 22, 39–43, 64–65
    comparable, 3–4, 40, 77, 103–105
    foreclosures on (*see* Foreclosures)
    locating potential, 39–50
    photographs of, 98–99, 100, 101
    property information sheets on,
        109–111
    repairs to/remodeling of, 107–108,
        174–179
    titles to, 104, 146–149 (*see also*
        Deed(s))
    wholesaling (*see* Wholesaling
        properties)
Property information sheets, 109–111
Purchase and sales contracts. *See*
    Contracts, sales
Purchase price. *See* Offers
Purchaser's statements, 85

Quitclaim deeds, 104

Real estate agents, 39–40, 84, 117,
    124–125
Real estate investing. *See also* Investors
    benefits of, 1–2
    as business, 10
    business structure in, 14–16, 84, 185
    creativity of deal structure in, 6–7
    learning about, 204–208
    office establishment and, 13–14
    preparation and, 16–17, 184–185
Real Estate Investors Association
    (REIA) groups, 39, 44–45, 67, 145
Real estate owned (REO), 22, 40
Rehabbers:
    assignment fees and, 194
    as buyers, 171–172, 198–199

closings and, 184, 186, 189–191, 197–200
deposits from, 41–43, 184, 186, 189–190
double closings with, 161, 191, 195, 196–200
investors as, 173–180
offer amounts and, 23–25, 172–173
proof of funds letters from, 126
seller occupancy and, 37
withdrawal of, 189–191
Relationships:
with bankers, 20, 117–119, 121
with buyers, 4
with family, 10–12, 36
with friends, 10–12
with sellers, 51–53, 186–189
Release Authorization, 73, 75, 79, 90, 113–114
Remodeling, 174–179
Rentals, 62–64, 65, 139, 180–182
Repairs list, 107–108, 174–175
Repayment plans, 61–62, 165
Roofs, 178–179

Safety, 57–58
Sales. *See also* Short-sales
contracts, 76, 79–80, 82, 84–86, 91–97, 170, 198
initiating, 53–59
of loans, 120
postponement of, 122, 162
sheriff's (*see* Foreclosures)
trustee, 151–152
Schedules, creating and maintaining, 9–10
Scott, Valerie, 2–5
Second/third mortgages, 131–132, 136–144, 147–149, 156
Self-promotion, 13–14, 44–46, 49–50
Sellers:
amounts owed by, 26, 195–196
bankruptcy of, 65, 91, 139, 144, 163–166
closings and, 183–184
contact with potential, 13, 43–44, 53–59

debt *vs.* ownership of, 146–149, 182
deficiency judgments and, 100–101
financial agreements with, 33–36
gratitude of, 4–5, 67, 88
hardship budgets from, 81
hardship letters from, 80, 88–91, 98, 141–143
hardship packages from, 123–124
investor as, 180
mortgages of (*see* Mortgages)
motivation of, 51–54, 173, 196
occupancy by, 36–38
options for, 59–65
relationship with, 51–53, 186–189
Release Authorization from, 73, 75, 79, 90, 113–114
sales contracts with, 76, 79–80, 82, 84–86, 92–97, 170, 198
"subject to" agreements with, 62–64, 139, 182
unethical investors and, 187–188
unsecured loans and, 139
withdrawal of, 186–189
Seller's statements, 86
Settlement letters, 26
Settlement statements, 31, 105, 194
Sheriff's sales. *See* Foreclosures
Short-sale packages:
comparable properties in, 3–4, 40, 77, 103–105
formal short-sale requests in, 75
hardship letters in, 80, 88–91, 98, 141–143
investor cover letters in, 42, 99–102, 139–142
to junior lien holders, 131
net sheets in, 105–107
photographs in, 98–99, 100, 101
property information sheets in, 109–111
Release Authorization in, 73, 75, 79, 90, 113–114
repairs list in, 107–108
sales contracts in, 76, 79–80, 82, 84–86, 91–97, 170, 198
submission to bank, 114

Short-sale packages (*Continued*)
  summary of contents, 69, 73
  telephone logs in, 74, 89
Short-sales:
  case study on, 2–6
  definition of, 19
  formal request for, 75
  reasons for, 21–23
Signage, 44, 45–47, 49–50
Signatures at closings, 185
Simultaneous closings, 161, 191, 195,
  196–200
Special warranty deeds, 104
State laws, 64, 149–152
Street signs, 44
"Subject to" agreements, 62–64, 139,
  182
Subprime adjustable-rate mortgages,
  156
Subsidized-housing programs, 181
Summary final judgments, 150

Tax advisers, 14–15
Tax liens, 153
Teaser adjustable-rate mortgages, 156
Telephone logs, 74, 89
Telephones, 13, 57, 115
Tenants, screening, 181–182

Testimonials, 2–4, 20, 33, 38, 47–49,
  66–68, 70–71, 97, 103, 125,
  132–135, 163, 167–168, 201–204
Thomas, Pete and Pamela, 70–88
341 hearings, 164–165
Title companies. *See* Closing agents
Title insurance, 198
Titles, property, 104, 146–149. *See also*
  Deed(s)
Title searches, 198
Training, 206
Trustee sales, 151–152

Unethical investors, 187–188
Unsecured loans, 139
Utilities, 174

VA (Department of Veterans Affairs)
  loans, 125, 155
Vehicle signs, 45–46

Wholesaling properties, 20, 23–25, 37,
  126–127, 161, 170–173, 191–196
Windows, 178
Writing, agreements in, 7–10, 15,
  159–160, 162, 163, 172

Yard maintenance, 174